HELL WITHIN HELL

Sexually Abused Child Holocaust Survivors

The Comorbidity of the Traumata

Rachel Lev-Wiesel
and
Susan Weinger

University Press of America,® Inc.
Lanham · Boulder · New York · Toronto · Plymouth, UK

Copyright © 2011 by
University Press of America,® Inc.
4501 Forbes Boulevard
Suite 200
Lanham, Maryland 20706
UPA Acquisitions Department (301) 459-3366

Estover Road
Plymouth PL6 7PY
United Kingdom

All rights reserved

British Library Cataloging in Publication Information Available

Library of Congress Control Number: 2011924080
ISBN: 978-0-7618-5477-7 (paperback : alk. paper)
eISBN: 978-0-7618-5478-4

In memory of my beloved parents Miriam (Martha) Cohen and Chaim (Laszlo) Wiesel—Holocaust survivors whom I deeply admire for their vitality and strength to grow out of ashes.

Rachel Lev-Wiesel

To those remarkable individuals who told or left untold their particular experiences of sexual abuse during the Holocaust.

Susan Weinger

TABLE OF CONTENTS

Preface	vii
Chapter 1: Introduction	1
Chapter 2: The Continuing Influence of Early Trauma	11
Chapter 3: Childhood Sexual Abuse	15
Marina	27
David	33
Condolisa	41
Judith	49
Cornelia	53
Dunia	59
Tova	69
Afterword	73
References	77
About the authors	83

PREFACE

As a daughter of two parents who survived the Holocaust as children, I was always interested in what they had gone through during *that* time. Yet, I was reluctant to ask my parents about their experiences because I sensed that it would be too painful for them to talk, and too much for me to hear. My parents often told me about their prewar family life, before my mother had been sent to Auschwitz, and my father, to Bergen Belsen. As with other children of Holocaust survivors, I didn't want my parents to tell me about their experiences in the concentration camps. It was too excruciating and frightening for me to deal with their personal stories. But as a child, after my parents had fallen asleep, I would turn on a flashlight that I'd hidden under the blanket, take out my library books and into the depths of the night I would read the biographies of Holocaust survivors. I admired my parents for their ability to carry on after surviving such atrocities. It was a wonderment to me how anyone could endure so much and remain sane and functional.

My personal interest expressed itself in my professional role as a clinical social worker treating Holocaust child survivors and their own children, commonly referred to as second-generation Holocaust survivors. Later, as a university faculty member I began to study the long-term psychological consequences of the Holocaust, including the positive psychological growth of survivors, referred to professionally as posttraumatic growth. My late colleague and friend, Professor Marianne Amir, and I, have published several studies on the impact of the Holocaust on child survivors. Listening to hundreds of interviews, we found some evidence of sexual abuse and decided to investigate further. Clearly, there was no way to evaluate the prevalence of sexual abuse during the Holocaust; but we did know that children were, are, and always will be a group at particular risk during wartime. We managed to recruit child survivors of the Holocaust who were willing to share their painful experiences of sexual abuse perpetrated by their non-Jewish "saviors", by strangers, or even (though rarely) by fellow Jews.

During a radio show dedicated to the long-term impact of the Holocaust, I invited survivors who had been sexually abused to be interviewed for a research study. Forty-two Holocaust survivors contacted us and volunteered to tell their stories. That study was the last one that Marianne and I wrote and published together before she died of cancer in January 2004.

Professor Susan Weinger, who is my colleague and friend, then agreed to join me in continuing this endeavor.

Rachel Lev-Wiesel

PREFACE

I am grateful for the chance to collaborate with Professor Rachel Lev in writing this book, because it gives us an opportunity to contribute to the literature about the Holocaust. With all that has been written concerning that time, stories of survivors who were sexually abused are rare. These stories need to be told now because the remaining survivors are elderly and their truth-telling cannot wait.

From the time I was a young girl, I remember the Holocaust being talked about as the horrific persecution of Jews. Such discussions were common in my family and in our community. The Holocaust was a backdrop of our everyday existence. As an adult, I recall discussing the impact of the Holocaust with a professor colleague of mine. He asked me whether I had personally experienced any anti-Semitism. His question took me aback. In a sense, how could the Holocaust—when Jews had been targeted for torture and murder—be anything else for me, as a Jewish woman, but personally anti-Semitic? As I pondered his question, I realized how deeply the impact of genocide has extended beyond the war years and how widely the ripples of its tidal wave continue to affect our people, and all people, generation after generation. The legacy of the Holocaust is also passed down, from those who actively or passively participated in this genocide, as well as from those who did everything possible to prevent the inhumanity.

Although the Holocaust affects each of us differently, we can collectively honor its survivors and value every one of their lives by reading their testimonies. For this reason, we decided to publish this book.

We are greatly in debt for the survivors' willingness to share with us their painful experiences and are in awe of their courage to come out and let the world hear their voices. We, their descendants have a commitment to make their stories known to the world.

Susan Weinger

Nota Bene:

To the greatest possible extent, we relayed the survivors' stories in their own words. We did not correct or probe into their childhood memories about the sequence of events, accuracy of dates, or lengths of time. Some stories are longer and more detailed than others. The interviews were conducted in a manner as to allow the survivors space to decide for themselves what life periods they wished to emphasize. We have changed the names of the survivors and other individuals mentioned by them in order to protect the privacy of our interviewees and those in their lives.

Our book provides background information about the Holocaust and its child survivors, the lasting impact of childhood trauma in general, and the effects of sexual abuse in particular. We then relate seven stories of child survivors who were sexually abused during the Holocaust. We end the book with personal reflections, but are careful to let the stories of these survivors stand on their own.

These individual stories recognize the fact that each survivor had a unique autobiography, and we will never know all of them. Grouping these people and their stories together may seem to deny them their own voices. They deserve to be treated individually so that their experiences and perceptions will be heard clearly, as an affirmation of all they have experienced. In sum, they merit being perceived as individuals rather than as being merely part of a group of people who had survived the same horrific time. Their loss and ours is that so many were not heard and never will be.

Telling their stories was not easy for the survivors. For some, the interview provided them with the first opportunity to speak of their Holocaust nightmares; for almost all, it was the first time they have described their sexual abuse. Every survivor was acutely aware that their experiences would finally be known and acknowledged. We are grateful to each of our interviewees for trusting us enough to share with us the atrocities they had endured. We are humbled in the face of their strength, their determination to live, their dignity, and their generosity in being able to give to others. Above all, they stand as a testament that the human spirit can overcome evil.

The authors thank Anat & Ofri Brin for their sensitive cover design which converges with the subject matter of our book.

Rachel Lev-Wiesel and *Susan Weinger*

CHAPTER 1:

INTRODUCTION

The Holocaust—historical background

The Nazi takeover of Germany in 1933 initiated the systematic, comprehensive, and obsessive state-sponsored persecution of all Jews. The sequential actions included forcing Jews to physically identify themselves by wearing a yellow star, stripping them of their possessions, citizenship and civil rights (Nuremberg Laws), removing them from civil service, business, academia, and the professions, and forcing them to emigrate. Lack of opposition from any other country enabled the Nazis to step forward with the "final solution"—a euphemism for the annihilation of six million Jews, including one and a half million children.

The Nazi genocidal machine aimed to not only methodically abolish all Jewish communities but also obliterate the procreative potential of the Jewish people. For this reason, Jewish children were targeted for immediate death. The flourishing communities of Warsaw, Riga, Salonika, and Amsterdam, just to mention a few, were destroyed, and hundreds of small communities vanished. From 1939 to 1945, Jews were slaughtered by Nazis, and in the case of some European countries, the Jews were slaughtered by their own countrymen who readily joined in the Nazi solution. For example, in Poland the citizenry fell into line with the Nazi persecution, and the Polish individuals who aided the Jews were the rare exception rather than the rule.

Ripped from family and community

Most Holocaust Survivors grew up in Jewish communities with rich cultural spirituality and communal structures. Unlike most child Survivors, adult Survivors had the experience of being an integral part of a cohesive community. Their families had established roots in the Jewish community, from which they developed their sense of belonging, security, and identification. Child Survivors old enough to participate in the life of the community also developed communal bonds, but they did not have the time to fully shape their personalities or identities. Survivors who were infants or toddlers at the beginning of the Holocaust were denied their entire childhood of parental care and community nurturing.

These Survivors did not have the opportunity to develop the bonds of belonging to a family and a community because they were torn away from their parents and communities; their childhood was violently ripped away from them.

The Nazi persecution of the Jews and the circumstances of war resulted in the forced separation of families, physical and psychological suffering, hunger, humiliation, and the frequent witnessing of brutality. Holocaust Survivors lost not only their families but also their religious, social and family traditions, along with their communities and a rich cultural heritage. They suffered a complete break with their pre-Holocaust lives and thus lost the basic sense of security, belonging and identity that family and community provide. One Survivor recalled thinking, "Even when we were liberated from Auschwitz, I did not want to leave, my entire family and friends were murdered there; I could not leave them there . . . where could I go . . . there was no one nowhere in the world to wait for me." Every Holocaust Survivor has a tragic personal and family history of loss.

Long lasting psychological consequences

There is consensus among mental health professionals that a significant disturbance in a child's sense of security, or their quality of life may have long-term impact. A stable relationship with a parental figure that meets the child's psychological and physical needs is crucial to ensure a lifelong psychological equilibrium (Klein, 1974; Krell, 1986, 1993; Winnicot, 1965). These stable conditions were unattainable for Jewish children from 1939 to 1945 in such countries as Poland, Czechoslovakia, France, Holland, and Hungary. Growing up without adequate food, insufficient shelter, extensive exposure to disease, exploitation and cruelty, the absence of trustful adults, a lack of love and care with no hope for a better future, had a lasting and intensified psychological impact on child Survivors. Researchers and clinicians regard the Holocaust as a constellation entailing specific psychological harm which increases in severity as the person ages (Chodoff, 1963; Davidson, 1992; Lederer, 1963; Niederland, 1964). Robinson, Rapaport-Bar-Sever and Rapaport (1994) studied 103 Child Survivors fifty years after the war and found that most Survivors continued to suffer from psychological distress symptoms and that their suffering is more severe than immediately after the war. Other recent studies (Amir & Lev-Wiesel, 2003) found a range of psychological distress symptoms among Survivors in general, such as poorer self-rated health in women and higher prevalence of Post Traumatic Stress Disorder (PTSD) among men (Landau & Litwin, 2000).

Survivor Syndrome

Niederland (1964) coined the term "survivor syndrome" to describe the combination of characteristic symptoms expressed by Holocaust Survivors. Survivor syndrome is complex and manifests itself in a variety of ways. Some Survivors had difficulties holding a job, maintaining relationships, or facing new situations. They also felt guilty for having survived. They exhibited bursts of anger, accompanied by a low frustration threshold, experienced feelings of helplessness, low self-esteem, and lack of initiative and interest in life, and endured sensations of being lost, along with anxiety attacks, and some psychosomatic symptoms.

According to Niederland, there are five main categories of "survivor syndrome": The first (1) is the death imprint, which refers to all forms of torture and gruesome images of death, such as the smell of smoke, the screams of the tortured, and the sights of misery. These imprints caused many of the Survivors to be trapped in time, unable to escape the torture they had witnessed and experienced. Because they are unable to escape these haunting, disturbing and gruesome images, they often are unable to sleep soundly or work with adequate concentration.

The second (2) category, Survivor's guilt, refers to feelings of remorse for the loved ones they lost and the burning question, "Why them and not me?" Guilt is one of the most common feelings among Survivors. Another type of guilt is a kind of reaction formation to the anger or hurt feelings of experiencing "abandonment" by their parents. Knowing that their parents had no other option and were helpless themselves when they turned them over to strangers "to be saved" or when the Nazis had forced their separation, they convert their angry feelings into guilt feelings. How can a child Survivor be angry at his or her unintentionally helpless parents who nonetheless succeeded in "saving" their child? The common result is the directing of anger toward oneself via guilt feelings.

The third category (3) is psychological numbing or not feeling of one's emotions, particularly positive feelings such as joy and happiness. Based on our clinical experience, we, the authors, wonder whether positive feelings are threatening to Survivors who believe they should have died along with their parents and that they have no right to feel joyful. Having positive feelings might seem to negate what the Survivor considers proper mourning for those they loved. Also, positive feelings might connect them more intimately with others; such need for connection is also threatening when those you love could be snatched away and harmed. However, some Survivors avoid all strong feelings, both positive and negative, protecting themselves from being entangled in any emotional interpersonal relationship even within their own families. Cutting off the experience of feelings yields protection from hurt.

Survivors also use this "tool" as a defense against overwhelming images. They not only block out feelings, but also the horrific memories of events, images, and cognitions that are intertwined with, and would tap into those emotions. One Survivor, for example, said that he was "born" at the age of six when he was brought to Israel after the war and adopted by a kibbutz family. When asked where he was born, he replies that he was born in a kibbutz.

Lorenzer's research (1968) studies of the psychological influence of the

Holocaust on Survivors dovetails with this aspect of psychological numbing. He noted that many Survivors rely heavily on the defense mechanism of denial (e.g., denial of having lost close family). This type of denial helped maintain psychological equilibrium through a rigid fixation (Nathan, Ettinger & Winnik, 1964). Survivors kept very firm, impermeable, mental boundaries. For example, they often succeeded in not talking about any of their experiences during the Holocaust. Even now, some talk about their own lives but skip over their five years of Holocaust trauma.

The fourth category (4) refers to a suspicious and paranoid attitude. Being persecuted as a Jew entailed not only physical, but also psychological abuse, and struck at the very core of the individual's worth as a human being. Hence, this legacy instilled a constant need to be guarded and watchful on emotional and psychological levels. This vigilance reduces the Survivor's ability to trust others and establish comfortable relationships. Security with anyone, including with their very young children, was denied to them. They invariably question the love of others toward them. Because they felt so profoundly abandoned, they cannot even trust their family members to be there; they are always prepared to, once again, be abandoned, emotionally and physically. Consequently, they are ultra-sensitive to criticism by even their closest family members. Even minor criticism might be an indication of their worthlessness, regardless of the age, closeness, or relation of the critic. They are very wary of any conflict with their children that might invite criticism, and they often respond to such conflict as if they were their children's age. Because of this, many children of Survivors learned not to criticize their parent(s), but instead, to be understanding toward them. They concealed their developmentally appropriate negative feelings, sensing that their parents are too sensitive to any sign of potential abandonment.

The fifth (5) category of the survivor syndrome concerns the search for meaning. Survivors need to find meaning in their own survival, in life itself and through the punishment of those who persecuted them. Being alive and surviving, in and of itself, meant that the Nazis had not totally destroyed their families and the Jewish people. Survival itself was a powerful act of resistance and revenge, and it demonstrated their strength and power to resist the Nazis. Being alive was a punishment to the Nazis, who were determined to exterminate all Jews. The Jews won on an individual level and as a group in terms of surviving and becoming founders of the State of Israel.

Birthing and raising children became the most important priority for the Survivors and the children became living memorial candles for lost family members (Vardi, 1991). The establishment of the State of Israel transformed the meaning of the Holocaust and served as the best proof of the Jewish victory over the Nazi extermination machine. The establishment of the State of Israel is a victory not only over the Nazis but over the whole world since other countries participated in the crime, either by murdering Jews or by refusing them asylum and leaving the Jews trapped in the executioner's multinational chambers. Jews survived the Nazis, and in the wake of the Holocaust, built and defended their own country. One child of Holocaust Survivors explained, "My parents saw me as a soldier, then an officer in the Israeli army, and vowed that this was the most meaningful aspect of their lives." Survivors were victorious because their children became strong and could be their defenders. Their children now have the means to defend them, themselves, and the succeeding generations, and they are not at risk of becoming a persecuted minority ever again. Child Survivors' parents could not defend them but they were able to give their children more security in the world than they had known. They provided their children a homeland that they will never have to flee.

Child Survivors are a distinct group

After the war and until the 1980s, those considered to be Survivors were exclusively those who had experienced the horrors of concentration or labor camps. In recent years, there has been greater recognition of the wide range of traumatic events that were experienced by individuals in the Nazi-controlled areas. While most Survivors were incarcerated in concentration camps, there were those who avoided imprisonment by hiding under false identities in monasteries, orphanages, Christian foster families, forests, or barns (Kestenberg & Brenner, 1986). Most of those Jews in hiding (experiencing the Holocaust outside of the camps) were children because they were more readily taken in by families and monasteries and it was their parents' priority to save them.

Holocaust child Survivors comprise a unique group of trauma victims who were exposed to prolonged stress and mass exposure in childhood, more than sixty years ago. Only recently have they been recognized as a distinguishable group of individuals who survived the war with different experiences from older Survivors. There are no exact statistics concerning the number of children who survived the Holocaust. After the war, approximately 50,000 child Survivors settled principally in Israel, but others immigrated to Canada, the United States, Belgium, and France (Tec, 1993).

Phases of deprivation experienced by Hidden Children

Dasberg (1990) conceptualized the period of childhood deprivation experienced by children in hiding, as divided into three main phases, or "traumatic sequences."

(1) The first sequence was during the pre-war and early war years when the child remained within the family and suffered from external anti-Semitic harassment, discrimination, ghettoization, and death threats. Parents, during this phase, were overburdened and frightened, and could no longer provide security for their children. Jews were prohibited from working and were robbed of their existing property, thus depriving them of financial means of survival. They risked their lives every time they stepped outside; their obvious presence, their mere existence invited violence. They were attacked in their own homes and could not ensure a safety zone for their children because police and others could force entry into their homes and arrest and beat them with impunity.

Parents were forced to put their children further into harm's way in an attempt to save them and their families. They were compelled to send their children, who would be less conspicuous than they would be as adults, outdoors, without the yellow badge in defiance of the persecutory mandate. The children would then forage for food, sell and buy in the black market, deliver messages, or collect information.

The vindictive societal, political, economic, and military forces made it impossible to fulfill the parental role and desire to protect their children. The children could no longer rely on their parents to make their world safe, and accordingly, the parents could not serve as an idealized image for as long as the children emotionally needed them to be so. The horrifyingly harsh external environment combined with the parents' Herculean efforts to help their families survive against all odds, caused parents to frequently feel desperate, depressed, frightened, and anxious. They were overwhelmed by their own emotional distress and they could not contain and sooth their children's distress. Sometimes a role reversal occurred, in which the children strived to meet their parents' emotional needs.

(2) The second sequence began after the breakup of the family, after its uprooting and final separation and transfer either to labor or concentration camps or into hiding within Christian families, monasteries, or forests. In this stage, children were suddenly dependent on non-parents, adult strangers who were often untrustworthy and thus, the children were exposed to other vagaries and terrors of persecution.

To arrive at this stage, the children first underwent the trauma of being separated from their parents. The first people children relate to are their parents, whose imprint and importance is engraved in their minds and hearts. Children's natural longing is to stay with their 'good enough' parents, no matter what happens. Indeed, they would prefer to die in their parents' embrace rather than be given away to strangers and try to survive by themselves.

But parents most often strived to save their children from the fires of extermination and desperately sought any rare opportunity to save them. The relatively small percentage of children whose parents were successful at finding a means of rescuing them nevertheless inherited a legacy of trauma.

Even though parents made desperate efforts to save their children, the children still perceived this life-saving separation as abandonment. Such separations occurred during times of crisis and usually involved a traumatic, pressured, rushed, forced, and severe severing from their parents and families of origin. Afterwards, the children were usually not given emotional support in mourning their enormous losses, not offered developmentally helpful explanations, and not soothed and comforted, nor were they provided with nurturing compensation and distractions. Following such a forced separation, the children usually wondered why their parents left them. They often became disoriented, angry, despondent, dissociative, withdrawn, distrusting, and felt that they themselves were to blame because they were unlovable and unworthy of living.

In contrast, the small percentage of children who had been abused within their own families received an emotionally corrective experience when their emergency parental figures turned out to be caring adults. Unfortunately, these homes were often temporary havens and the children lost them as well. The hidden children perceived that their biological parents did not want them and that subsequently, neither did the nurturing substitutes who had given them refuge. The message that they were not good enough for anyone, reverberated within this group of children. They regarded themselves as deserving all sorts of punishment and undeserving of life itself.

Sometimes parents turned their children over to a monastery in order to save their lives at the cost of erasing their heritage. These children were trained for converting to Christianity and denied an opportunity to be raised within their own culture. They not only lost everything familiar to them–their parents, siblings, extended families, friends, neighborhoods, schools, synagogues, and their religious and cultural way of life–but also had the quality and viability of their memories stripped from them. They were often told that their parents were bad people and as Jews, death and torture were due to them. They could not tell anyone in the monastery that they missed their parents or that they were lonely as it was sacrilegious to yearn for connection with a Jew. Who should they trust? Should they trust their parents whom they had loved but who were perhaps bad people? Were their memories only a delusional trick? Should they trust people in the monastery who negated their past and their origins? These children in the monasteries found it necessary to conceal their true identity of being born Jewish, so that they would not be exposed and forcibly taken to a concentration camp. Their loneliness increased in having to hide their Jewish origins; an effort which denied them relationships involving spontaneous and open communication.

(3) The third sequence began at liberation. The re-entry into post-war society and transformation into being post-war adults was decisive for the outcome of the entire traumatic sequence. For many, childhood deprivation was intense during this period because of the confrontation with massive losses, chaotic post-war conditions, new forms of neglect, and their refugee status. Finding relatives and friends who had survived the terror was critical to their adjustment. Whether or not the children received social, emotional, and concrete support also influenced their adaptation. Another factor was whether or not they could find a new meaning for their lives.

After liberation, some children wandered through Europe searching for relatives. Many struggled through arduous and long journeys to return to their hometowns. Most faced major disappointment in discovering that their family had perished; their homes were taken by others; while local, primarily Christian residents, often brutally rejected them. Their houses had been confiscated by their neighbors who wanted them to disappear, not challenge their ownership and remind them of their criminal and immoral behaviors. Not only did these children suffer humiliation, cruelty, and hunger during the war, but their old neighbors did not welcome them back nor were they happy about the fact that they had survived the war. These child Survivors were again faced with having to survive difficult circumstances, but this time with diminishing hope that their parents, relatives, friends, or Jewish acquaintances from their previous life had survived the inferno.

Those select children who found one of their parents or relatives alive also had unforeseen hurdles to overcome. Their delight at finding a parent or a relative was often followed by disappointment and disillusionment. The relative or parent, who most likely suffered PTSD, was not in any physical or mental shape to support the child. They needed the child to understand what they had gone through and why they were depleted of emotional resources. The child Survivors often understood their parents' internal conflict to a degree, but simultaneously they felt anger at their parent(s) for deserting them and not being fully available upon their reunion. The children had clung to an idealized image of their parents, and approached their parents with the hope of being a child again and receiving what they had missed. But the parents were not the same parents after the war. With both the children and the parents suffering from PTSD, neither party found the support in each other that they so needed.

After the war, Jewish agencies aimed to rescue these children. They diligently searched for them and gathered them from Christian families and from the camps to be brought to Israel or to the United States. The children did not always want to be transported but they were not given any choice. The law dictated that the children were to be returned to the Jewish community through its representative agencies. There was no information available about the experiences of these children to guide the Jewish agencies in their work. The mission was to take them from the hell they had experienced and offer them a new life in a place where such a catastrophe would not befall them again. Those children fortunate enough to have been fostered by nurturing families did not want to be uprooted from their homes. This was re-traumatizing and a reverberation of the first trauma of separation from their biological parents. Furthermore, they and other hidden children, as well as children from the camps, often did not want to be reacquainted with Judaism or reintegrated into the Jewish community. In their minds, being a Jew meant death, torture, and immense discrimination. They were faced with having to come to terms with a religion and an identity that had been demonized and would continue to be a threat to them.

Children rescued by Jewish agencies and transported to Israel were presented with extraordinary challenges. They had to learn a new language in a new country with multicultural influences. They had to become Jews again and adapt to difficult survival conditions in Israel before the War of Independence. During the war, their lives and the lives of their friends and companions were endangered.

The social pressures involved in creating a new state exacerbated their adjustment challenges. They were not supposed to talk about what they were going through. Jews in Palestine were focused on establishing the State of Israel and did not want to look back. They strived to build a country in which Jews could stand tall, free from the indignities of humiliation and annihilation. But these Palestinian Jews had also internalized the world's raging anti-Semitism and so regarded European Jewry as weak and ready victims. To make matters worse, they blamed the Survivors for remaining in Europe and not immigrating to Israel before the *Shoah* (Holocaust). Thus, these formerly hidden children felt ashamed and acquiesced to their shame by keeping their feelings and concerns to themselves.

Nonetheless, coming to the Israel and being a part of the building of a Jewish state provided hope and meaning to the lives of many of the Survivors. When child Survivors, alone or with the their found parent(s), prepared to immigrate to Israel, the new challenges facing them and the hope for the establishment of the State gave their lives meaning and provided them with a possibility for post-traumatic growth. They felt the revitalization of starting a new life in their own country and pride in proving to the world and to themselves that the Nazis could not destroy all of their families or the entire Jewish people.

CHAPTER 2:

THE CONTINUING INFLUENCE OF EARLY TRAUMA

Children's age and place of hiding made a difference

Most studies view the Holocaust as an inclusive single event, rather than a period of time that comprised different types of traumatic experiences. However, in recent years there has been greater recognition that a wide range of traumatic events were experienced by individuals in the Nazi-controlled areas, both in concentration camps and while avoiding capture by hiding under false identity in monasteries, orphanages, Christian foster families, forests or in barns (Kestenberg & Brenner, 1986). Research demonstrates that the age and specific circumstances of the individual during the war were critical.

It has become increasingly clear that a victim's age at the time of exposure to a traumatic event is of importance for the long-term consequences. Tec (1993) points out that those who were children during the war were forced to endure formidable stressors without the benefit of adult coping resources and adaptations. Gampel (1992) emphasizes that these children were forced to function as adults in a world gone mad.

Some studies that examined psychological distress in relation to Holocaust Survivors' personal experience, reported that Holocaust Survivors who were not in concentration camps had fewer global psychiatric symptoms compared to Holocaust Survivors who were in labor and concentration camps (Eaton, Sigal, & Weinfeld, 1982). Furthermore, Robinson, Rapaport-Bar-Sever, and Rapaport (1994) found that Survivors of death camps suffered more from depression and anhedonia than those who experienced other forms of persecution by the Nazis. They also found that child Survivors of death camps over the long term were less able to cope and adjust compared to child Survivors who experienced other forms of persecution.

When Yehuda, Schmeidler, and Siever, et al., (1997) compared Holocaust Survivors in concentration camps to those who were in "hiding" during the war, they discovered different findings. Although the experience setting (concentration camp vs. hiding) was not associated with different PTSD patterns, the younger the child's age, the greater number of stressful events correlated with serious symptoms of psychogenic amnesia, hypervigilance, and emotional detachment.

Lev-Wiesel and Amir (2004) examined the impact of the setting of the Holocaust experience on the subsequent levels of PTSD, psychological symptoms of distress, personal resources, and quality of life experienced by child Survivors. Generally they found that there were no differences in the levels of post traumatic stress disorder (PTSD) between Survivors who had been prisoners in concentration camps and others who had been in hiding. However, Survivors who had been in Catholic Christian institutions usually suffered less PTSD than Survivors hidden by gentile families. Survivors who were hiding in the woods and/or with partisans had less intrusive memories of the terror than Survivors in other settings of hiding. Those hiding with the partisans managed to preserve their self-esteem, identity, and physical strength. The authors explained that children who hid among orphans in Catholic institutions had to become Catholic, thereby forfeiting their Jewish identity and constantly being forced to hide any signs of their former religion. These children, by having to hide important aspects of themselves, needed to avoid intimacy and attachment with both adults and other children. Instead, they sought comfort in the required prayer to Jesus and the mandatory Catholic rituals.

Survivors who were captured and imprisoned in concentration camps stopped hiding. The rules of the camp were very clear. Death was often regarded as a satisfactory remedy for the daily horror prisoners endured. Hiding in the woods and/or being with partisans meant being on the run from place to place, starvation, thirst, and cold, living in a constant uncertainty regarding the present, and endangering life in order to procure basic needs. Partisans were proactive which meant that, to a certain degree, they were in control of their lives. It seems that doing something active to cope with life threats and thus surviving, helped preserve those Survivors' self-confidence, self-control, and self-appreciation. Having been in a foster family was found in the Lev-Wiesel and Amir study (2004) to be associated with the most severe long-term distress compared to other hiding settings. According to the Survivors testimonies, some foster families were nurturing and warm, and provided healthy, happy lives to the children. However, others were cruel and harsh, strengthening feelings of fear, loneliness, and helplessness in the children dependent on and indebted to them. Being turned over to foster families, often by the child's parents themselves, and forced to accept a new identity, as well as later, after the war, being compelled to once again become a Jew (which was perceived as dangerous) might have harmed the children's basic sense of belonging and self-identity. Belonging, as well as feeling secure and protected, are basic needs of any human being (Maslow, 1968). Lack of satisfaction of these basic needs is likely to cause high levels of frustration, anxiety, and depression. These situations harm self-esteem and self-reliance as well as increase anger and hostility.

Long-term consequences of early Holocaust trauma

Regardless of the fact that after the War, the majority of child Survivors managed to live normal and creative lives (Krell, 1993), a number of qualitative studies dealing with PTSD symptoms and adaptation strategies used by child Survivors, suggest that most child Survivors still suffer from symptoms of the Survivor Syndrome (Breiner, 1996; Kestenberg & Brenner, 1996; Krell, 1993; Mazor & Mendelson, 1998; Moskovitz & Krell, 1990; Robinson, Rapaport-Bar-Sever, & Rapaport, 1994; Tauber & Van-Der-Hal, 1997). Kestenberg (1992, 1993) claimed that child Survivors adopt psychological defenses such as numbing of their feelings; they view the world and others in black and white, and frequently suffer from depression, phobias and distorted self-image. Others emphasized that the most outstanding psychological effects of persecution are loss of identity and feeling worthless (Brenner, 1988; Bunk & Eggers, 1993; Rustow, 1989), accompanied by a lifelong sense of bereavement (Mazor & Mendelsohn, 1998).

Self-identity in the shadow of the Holocaust

The concept of personal identity refers to an inner sense of wholeness and security which is achieved when there is continuity between the individual's perception of self and others' perceptions of him/her (Erikson, 1968). Personal identity is the outcome of identifications with significant others and developmental processes that begin in infancy and continue through adulthood. Identification plays a central role in the individual's ability to form relationships (Klein, 1976). If the process of identification is arrested or sabotaged, there may be long-term detrimental effects on the individual. Such effects may include poor quality of life and a weakened personality structure (Jensen, Huber, Cundick & Carlson, 1991).

A study conducted by Lev-Wiesel and Amir (2004) that examined the impact of lost identity on Holocaust child Survivors' psychological well-being in adulthood, revealed that not knowing one's original identity did not lead to greater levels of PTSD. But Survivors with lost identity suffered from lower physiological and psychological health and exhibited more aspects of depression and anxiety.

Not knowing one's identity appeared to be associated with more complaints about physical pain and poor health. The fact that Holocaust Survivors, in general exhibit heightened levels of somatic complaints (e.g., Bower, 1994, Stermer, Bar and Levy, 1991) as well as higher levels of chronic pain (Yaari, Eisenberg, Adler and Birkhan, 1999) has been noted earlier. Other research has shown that high degrees of somatization are often associated with very early psychological injury, such as sexual abuse (Bell, 1994). This suggests that somatizing behavior among adults derives, in part, from childhood. Stuart and Noves (1999) indicated that anxious attachment behavior derives from childhood experiences with caregivers. According to them, when under stress as adults, somatizers use physical complaints to elicit care. Holocaust child Survivors who were stripped of their identity were anxious to form human bonds and consequently, they somatized during adulthood. In addition, it seems that child Survivors perceive their body as the only continuous, existing identity and the only clear evidence they have of their original identity; so they must vigilantly guard it.

This theory is in line with van der Kolk's (1999) research on the biology of PTSD, which suggests that there are persistent and profound alternations in stress hormone secretion and memory processing in patients with PTSD. According to van der Kolk (1999) the body seems to remember the trauma even if the mind seems to forget. Yehuda, McFarlene, and Shalev (1998) also suggested that the development of PTSD may be facilitated by an atypical biological response in the immediate aftermath of a traumatic event (in this case it may be the separation from the parents) which in turn leads to a maladaptive psychological state.

Understanding about this specific population of Holocaust child Survivors who lost their identity, can be gathered from the study of adoption. Most studies on children's adjustment have concluded that adopted children have increased problems, at least during middle childhood and early adolescence (Brodzinsky, 1993). When examining studies focusing on the search process among adult adoptees (Schecter and Bertocci, 1990), it can be concluded that the need to know about one's birth origin can be quite significant. The motivation for this search is complex, but is essentially grounded in feelings of loss and disconnectedness from one's origin. In this sense, the psychology of adoptees and Holocaust survivors who were separated from their families at an early age has some similarities, although the outcome for the latter group is clearly more affected by the trauma and atrocities they have experienced.

CHAPTER 3:

CHILDHOOD SEXUAL ABUSE

Definition of Childhood Sexual Abuse

The World Report on Violence and Health (Krug, Mercy, Dahlberg & Zwi, 2002) defines sexual abuse as "any sexual act, attempt to obtain a sexual act, unwanted sexual comments or advances, or acts to traffic a person's sexuality, using coercion, threats of harm or physical force, by any person regardless of relationship to the victim, in any setting, including but not limited to home and work" (p. 149). Childhood Sexual Abuse (CSA) is defined as any sexual act between an adult and a child in which the child is used for the sexual satisfaction of the perpetrator (Briere, 1992). CSA can take different forms such as requesting sexual favors, sexual advances, any other verbal or nonverbal conduct of a sexual nature, sexual bullying—such as grabbing and/or insults, as well as sexual activity that involves violence or intimidation.

Any sexual act with a child is always sexual abuse. There is no such thing as consensual sex with a child, because a child is too young developmentally and/or too dependent on the perpetrator to give true consent. The child may not be physically mature enough for sex, and surely not emotionally. Children naturally trust adults to protect them. Sexual abuse confuses them and destroys their trust, especially if they love the adults involved, or even if they enjoy the touching. There are cases in which the sexual exploitation of a child by an adult is conducted with what appears at first to be warmth and love. The child, who is often dependent on the exploiter, is either led to believe that this a legitimate expression of love or that he or she must comply in order to keep the adult's love and protection.

Children learn from their exploiters that they themselves are to blame for their abuse. Sometimes, children who are exploited in these as-if-love relationships might become sexually aroused. The perpetrators lead the children to believe that they are being sexually exploited because of their own needs rather than those of the abusers. Typically, this distortion remains with the victim for years. One adult survivor continued to regard herself as the seducer and the one responsible for her abuse when she revealed to her therapist, "If I was not such a beautiful girl, this man wouldn't have done what he did to me." In her mind, it was her fault for being beautiful.

But of course, these manipulated and violated children are the victims. Children have no responsibility for sexual abuse, even when they feel that they themselves were the seducers. They are not responsible for what adults ask them to do, especially when an adult is responsible for them as in the role of a parent or guardian. The need for parental love is so overriding that a child will do anything to secure that love, even if the child does not want to do something or if it harms the child to do it. Furthermore, children understand that they should keep the abuse a secret and not talk about it even if the perpetrator never asks them to do so. They are afraid of telling anyone because it might mean that they would be punished by or even deserted by this adult. They are trapped in the abuse.

Childhood sexual abuse is considered to be a unique severe traumatic event since it includes violation of the child's body. Most sexually abused survivors consider sexual abuse the most traumatic event they could have experienced. When both physical and sexual abuses were involved, survivors usually cite their experiences of sexual abuse as the more traumatic, especially if the abuse occurred during childhood (Frazier et al., 1997; Resnick, Kilpatrick, Dansky, Saunders, & Best, 1993). Unlike other forms of abuse such as physical abuse, in which the violation is on the skin or surface of the child's body (whether or not internal injuries are caused), sexual abuse denotes oral, anal, or genital penetration (DiLillo et al., 2006). Following sexual abuse, the child's body can no longer be perceived as a "safe home." Victims become homeless within their own bodies because their bodies no longer belong to them, but feel as though they have been taken over by the perpetrator. Filled with hatred toward their bodies, they no longer want to live within them, but neither can they leave their bodies because that would mean having to die.

Feeling torn apart by this internal rift is not something generally experienced by children who have been physically abused. In contrast, those who have been sexually abused express disgust toward their own bodies and feel they cannot achieve a level of adequate "cleanliness". No matter how much they want to flee their bodies, they cannot disconnect from them. One patient, for example, had been sexually abused by her father since she was three years old—first orally, then anally, and later vaginally as she reached her preteen years. The young woman told her counselor that her violated body felt as if it no longer belonged to her; she hated its very existence. She attempted to cut off her nipples because her perpetrator salaciously delighted in them. In attempting to clean her body, which she thought was sullied from the abuse she repeatedly drank cleaning fluids and had to be hospitalized.

Sexual abuse victims often use a coping mechanism known as dissociation to deal with their trauma. Dissociation refers to a mental process that produces a lack of connection in the person's thoughts, memories, feelings, actions, or sense of self (American Psychiatric Association, 1994). To create this disconnection, the victim unconsciously uses defensive functions such as creating automatic behaviors, responding to overwhelming stimuli, escaping from life stressors and despair, compartmentalizing catastrophic events, seeking cathartic relief from certain feelings, avoiding and relieving pain, and altering the sense of self so that the traumatic event is experienced as if "it hadn't happened" to them" (Putnam, 1993). According to Silberg (1998), sexually abused children tend to dissociate themselves during a traumatic event. This state allows the child to survive and protect his or her functioning self as much as possible (Krystal et al., 2000; Midgley, 2002). Through this mechanism, abused children can temporarily avoid the full onslaught of their pain and suffering. Escaping the abusive situation can often be possible only virtually in the victim's mind, whereas the body continues to suffer (Silberg, 1998). As a result, through dissociation, victims are able to block out certain aspects of reality so they do not have to be fully aware of the devastating danger and pain they are actually experiencing. Indeed, if they were totally cognizant of their inescapable peril, it would likely overwhelm their mental processes. Dissociation permits the complete blocking out of reality in the effort to hold on to one's sanity.

Dina, a Holocaust child survivor, exemplified this dissociation process, in which certain information known to a person is not associated with other information as it would normally be (Somer & Somer, 1997). She spoke about her horrific experience in the labor camp, where she was molested by one of the guards. During the first meeting with the interviewer, Dina said that her mother and sister were with her in the labor camp for the entire time period and that she shared all her feelings and experiences with them. She credited this intimate sharing with having saved their lives. But during a second interview, Dina revealed that she could not remember who was with her during the time she was abused, nor did she remember if she told anyone about it. She had compartmentalized the sexual abuse, containing it in her mind as separate from other associations, which led to the disparity in her statements.

Dissociation had enabled Martha, also a Holocaust survivor, to tear her feelings apart from her mental knowledge of suffering in Auschwitz. Martha's feelings were so divorced from what she knew to be true that she felt compelled to watch television programs about the Holocaust. Her dissociation kept her mental awareness unconnected from her feelings. Martha explained that she felt driven to watch these frightening movies because, although she knew she survived Auschwitz, she did not actually feel the experience of having been there. She hoped that by watching these television programs, she could affectively reconnect to these places and experiences so that she could emotionally accept that she was there. It is disconcerting and disorienting to have one's feelings and thoughts kept separate, when an integrated and whole sense of oneself requires that they be united.

As a defense mechanism, while dissociation may protect against absorbing the full impact of immediate experiences, it comes at high personal costs. This defense that best protected abused children during traumatic times also makes it more difficult for them to establish satisfying relationships. Individuals who were sexually abused in early childhood or adolescence show greater impairment in human relationships (Swartz, 2002). Children are not born with a developed sense of who they are and with full-fledged personalities. They learn instead about themselves through their interactions with others. Based on how significant persons in their lives treat them, they internalize images of themselves and of others. From these early relationships, children learn how they and others are to be in relationships with one another and carry these expectations into other relationships in their lives. By having a solid trusting relationship(s) with a parent(s), the child develops inner perceptions of self and others as pleasurable, dependable, and trustworthy human beings. In contrast, child Survivors of the Holocaust often received a grossly distorted blueprint of what relationships offer and who they and others are.

Dissociation also fragments the self (Shengold, 1989). To dissociate from the horrors of an experience, children minimize the abuse and take the blame. Minimizing the abuse, along with self-blaming, contributes to the development of dissociative mechanisms, just as these factors are simultaneously reinforced by the dissociation. In an attempt to mentally pare down the experience and also stay safer by blaming oneself rather than directing anger toward the violent perpetrator, the child pushes aspects of the violations away from conscious awareness. The pressure not to see, not to hear, and not to speak prevents the victimized child from processing the experience so that the child is less able to verbally describe what happened.

Dissociation becomes pervasive even in situations that are not dangerous. Whenever victims or survivors encounter any stimuli that might unconsciously be associated with the abuse, they once again dissociate. They tend to dissociate more and more because there are so many stimuli that become associated with the abuse. For example, if they meet another adult who in any way resembles the abuser, they dissociate, or, the minute they feel that they might get into an intimate relationship, they might dissociate as well. Dissociation helps them not to feel, so they become more and more numb and freer from pain. However, this state of deadened feelings prevents them from experiencing intimacy in relationships. They might engage in a sexual-loving relationship, but they are not truly present. They do not have access to their loving feelings and the joy of being so wondrously connected to another human being.

Dissociation can even have a negative impact on the learning abilities of child victims and survivors. Intrusive flashbacks and dissociation can result in a lack of concentration and memory that causes learning difficulties. Sometimes children or adult survivors alternate between functioning at a high level of skill and intelligence and much lower levels of competency. At one moment, they are perceived by others as being bright and capable people, and at another as being unable to function and think competently. This unnatural variability confuses teachers, employers, family, and friends and results in their inconsistent responses toward these children. The children become confused by the contradictory messages given to them, and their self-esteem may plummet even further.

Dissociation spurs other unhealthy coping strategies such as identification with the aggressor; identification with the other parent's apparent passivity, silent collaboration or lack of awareness, or identification with the victimized self. When children identify with their aggressors, they incorporate aggressive behaviors that belittle the rights of others, making it possible for survivors of abuse to become perpetrators themselves. When children identify with what appears to them to be the other parent's passivity or lack of awareness, they may also turn a blind eye to the suffering of others. Lastly, when children perceive themselves as victims, they continue to act in ways that are expected by their perpetrators. It is no wonder that many children exploited as prostitutes have been sexually abused within their own families.

These unhealthy coping mechanisms, stemming from dissociation, may encourage an individual to engage in hazardous situations while blocking out the inherent risks or need for safety precautions. Abuse victims may not be able to access their feelings of fear. In this way, dissociation can prevent them from picking up cues about risks in life. Rather than heeding warning signs and avoiding dangerous situations, they may be more likely to get hurt again. Lora, a Holocaust child Survivor, who was taught by her "savior" to seduce male adults, often invited male strangers to her home. She explained that she responded to what she saw as the "need in their faces." She continued inviting strangers to her home even after she was robbed three times.

These unhealthy coping strategies intensify with the destructive environmental situation in which a child lives. The terrifying environment of the Holocaust provoked the dissociative processes in the children's minds. Perpetrators of sexual abuse rob children of their independence even in the best of environmental situations. During the Holocaust, children were extremely dependent on their saviors for survival, some of whom were the very people who had become their abusers. They lived with the threat that they could be turned over to the Nazis, who were more frightening to them than their sexual abusers. These children were effectively trapped, with dissociation as their only escape valve. The helplessness stemming from being doubly trapped by the threat of the Nazis and the betrayal of caregivers served to reinforce the children's avoidance of thought, feeling, or action, thus providing an additional catalyst for the development and intensification of their dissociative disorders (Silberg, 1998). The severity of the dissociative symptoms may vary depending on factors such as age of abuse onset, severity of abuse, emotional closeness or dependence on the abuser, dysfunction of early social environment, and psychological factors (Gold et al., 1999). Clearly, all these factors concurred during the Holocaust in a way that could generate severe dissociative symptoms in these children.

Effects of Sexual Abuse in Childhood

The age at which rape and/or sexual molestation occurs appears to be critical in how a child victim reacts to such abuse. When children are sexually abused at very early ages, they believe that that is the nature of relationships between adults and children. They regard themselves as merely sex objects whose role it is to seduce adults they encounter. When the child is already an adolescent at the time the sexual abuse occurs, the child knows what a relationship with an adult should be. An adolescent understands that it is a distorted relationship and is more likely to escape it when and if possible. The consequence to the adolescent is hatred of one's own body. Teenagers begin to hate their own bodies because these have betrayed them by letting the perpetrators in. It is no wonder that self-loathing and viewing oneself as a sex object leads sexually abused children and adolescents to engage in self-destructive behaviors such as self-mutilation or risky sex (Rodrigues-Srednicki, 2001). The negative self-regard and greater use of dissociation that abuse victims experience apparently affect their awareness of danger cues and their willingness to be in potentially dangerous situations throughout their lives (Zelikovsky & Lynn, 2002).

Sexual abuse at a young age is likely to result in more severe forms of PTSD than other forms of abuse (Frazier, Byrne, Glaser, Hurliman, Iwan, & Searles, 1997; Kilpatrick, Saunders, Amick-McMullen, & Best, 1989; Ullman & Filipas, 2001). Persons with PTSD exhibit such symptoms as hyperarousal, avoidance of anything that reminds them of the abuse, and wariness. Some sexually abused children manage to avoid developing PTSD because of factors such as personal resources, social support, or sexual abuse that was less severe or painful or that occurred at an older age. However, even if sexually abused children circumvented all the symptomatology of PTSD, they are still likely to have dissociation. Findings such as those of Kendall-Tackett, Meyer-Williams, and Filkenhore (1993) and Rind, Tromovitch, and Bauserman (1998) report that up to 49 percent of sexually abused children showed no posttraumatic stress symptoms. However, about 80 percent of adult survivors of childhood sexual abuse actually have dissociative disorders (Van Den Bosch, Verheul, & Van Den Brink, 2003). Shalev (1993) has suggested that the initial dissociative reactions of victims of traumatic events become entrenched, especially if these events occurred in childhood.

Dissociation, employed by the individual as a result of the overwhelming amount of panic and psychological arousal caused by the trauma, may prevent him or her from emotionally processing the external cues associated with the trauma (Shalev, 1997). Thus, dissociation may lead to the development of symptoms of PTSD (Foa & Kozak, 1986) and to pathological fear structures such as phobias, fear of going outside because everyone is dangerous, or reluctance to talk to anyone because of lack of trust. Research focusing on the individual psychopathology associated with childhood sexual abuse found that such abuse carries a high risk of triggering most disorders, such as PTSD, suicidal tendencies, depression, anxiety, low self-esteem, obsessive-compulsive disorders, phobias, paranoid ideation, substance abuse, eating disorders, personality disorders, and dissociation (Fleming, Mullen, Sibthorpe, & Bammer, 1999; Simpson & Miller, 2002).

Peleikis, Mykletum, and Dahl (2003), who examined the relative influence of child sexual abuse and family background risk factors on the risk for mental disorders, found that individuals who were sexually abused after the age of 16 reported more anxiety disorders and depression than those who were abused at a younger age. However, the vast majority of individuals who develop dissociative disorders have documented histories of repetitive, overwhelming, and often life-threatening trauma at a sensitive developmental stage of childhood, usually before the age of nine (Draijer & Langeland, 1999; Zurbriggen & Freyd, 2004). Other studies examining the associations of childhood traumatic experiences and childhood neglect with dissociative experiences and PTSD indicated that dissociation scores as well as PTSD scores were higher among those with history of childhood sexual abuse. This was particularly true among those who reported having experienced intra-familial sexual abuse before the age of 16 (Van Den Bosch, Verheul, Langwland, & Van Den Brink, 2003). The fact that individuals who were sexually abused in early childhood or adolescence showed greater impairment in object relations (Swartz, 2002) and were engaged more in self-destructive behaviors such as self-mutilation or risky sex than others (Rodrigues-Srednicki, 2001) has been explained by the increase in dissociative experiences (Zelikovsky & Lynn, 2002). Hoyt (2002) suggested that the use of dissociation impairs the victims' awareness of danger cues and increases their willingness to participate in potentially dangerous situations throughout their lives.

Effects of Childhood Sexual Abuse in Adulthood

Reviews of the vast array of studies examining the long-term effects of childhood sexual abuse enumerate a wide variety of psychological, behavioral, and social difficulties in adults. Symptoms range from depression and poor self-esteem to interpersonal difficulties, substance abuse, and personality disorders (Finkelhor, 1990; Moeller, Bachmann, & Moeller, 1993; Neumann, Houskamp, Pollock, & Briere.1996; Royse, Rompf, & Dohooper, 1991). A recent unpublished study conducted by Gal, Levav, and Gross, indicated that exposure to sexual or physical abuse during childhood before age 13 is an important risk factor for mood and anxiety disorders in adulthood, as well as for higher psychological distress.

Numerous studies have addressed the feelings that survivors of childhood sexual abuse hold toward themselves (Bruckner & Johnson, 1987; Derek, 1989). Extremely low self-esteem or self-hatred is common (Briere, 1989; Russel, 1986). Survivors often seize the distorted belief that they are responsible for the abuse perpetrated against them, which results in patterns of self-blaming. Many abusers tell children that it is their fault that they have been abused, shifting the blame away from themselves and placing it squarely on the children (Bass & Davis, 1988; Derek, 1989).

Not surprisingly, since symptoms of PTSD and depression were found to be associated with physical health conditions (for example, Kendall-Tackett, 2002), women CSA survivors were found also to suffer, more than others, from health problems such as cardiovascular symptoms (Farley & Patsalides, 2001), gastrointestinal complaints (Leserman, 2005), diabetes (Kendall-Tackett & Marshall, 1999), arthritis and physical disability (Leserman, 2005), somatization and general unexplained pain disorders (Randolph & Reddy, 2006). In the gynecological realm, CSA survivors suffer more chronic pelvic pain than non-CSA women (Nijenhuis et al., 2003), sexual dysfunction (Reissing, Binik, Khalife, Cohen & Amsel, 2003), painful menstruation, and vaginal discharge (Pikarinen, Saisto, Schei, Swahnberg & Halmesmaki, 2007).

Childhood Sexual Abuse During the Holocaust

Little is currently known about child sexual abuse survivors who also endured the Holocaust. Childhood sexual abuse has always, and still is, a difficult topic to discuss openly. In addition, the domain of Holocaust atrocities has been difficult for society to address. The combination of two painful issues and emotional burdens, childhood sexual abuse and Holocaust atrocities, has created an invisible barrier in both studying and discussing these intertwined topics. Jewish children during the war were completely dependent on their sexual persecutors, who were often the adults who hid them and ostensibly saved their lives. As a result, the effects of sexual abuse might be expected to be particularly traumatic for children in the overriding circumstances of persecution and fear.

During the war years, some Jewish children felt abandoned by their parents, even if they were old enough to understand that their mothers and fathers had struggled to save them by finding caretakers for them. In turn, they experienced guilt for their feelings and for harboring resentment against their parents. Jewish children in hiding were alone and extremely lonely. The support children might benefit from during "normal" times was absent during the Holocaust. Family closeness, availability of extended family, and high-functioning adult role models such as teachers were not present. Children lacked parents and other adults to turn to who might have protected them by talking with them and teaching them that their bodies are their own.

Sometimes the children internalized anti-Semitism and even agreed with their perpetrators that they themselves deserved to suffer and were meant to endure the abuse. According to some survivors, they learned during that virulently active anti-Semitic period that being Jewish predestined them for abuse. Some would identify with their perpetrators and would harm themselves by mutilation. Such identification led them to believe that they could become less tainted, dirty, and evil by enduring more pain. The path to greater purity was to undergo greater torment.

Those children who experienced strong identification with their perpetrators were likely to experience confusion because of the extreme dangers posed by the Holocaust. They were loyal and grateful to their saviors but felt the incongruous sense that sexual abuse was wrong and hurtful to themselves.

Some child Survivors told of having been raped by partisans, Russian soldiers who freed the camps, Ukrainians who targeted women hiding in the woods, or by camp guards. Still others told horrible stories of having been used for experimental laboratory tests including forced sexual relations with siblings and parents. Ringelheim (1998) emphasized the sexual vulnerability of Jewish girls and women at the time of the Holocaust, as well as the persistent silence that has surrounded this topic. She questioned whether this silence reflects the reluctance of Survivors to reveal their experiences or the reluctance of researchers to hear them.

One reason for the scarcity of clinical and empirical reports regarding childhood sexual abuse during the Holocaust may lie in the embarrassment Survivors felt when sharing these humiliating experiences with others. They grew up in an age and in a society in which sex in intimate relationships, let alone sexual abuse, was not discussed. It is only recently that people have begun speaking publicly about sexual abuse. In fact, only in recent years are women who receive treatment for domestic violence asked if the violence includes being raped by their husbands or lovers. Traditionally, it has been easier in many societies to face the realities of physical battering than of sexual abuse.

Similarly, Israeli society and Jews in the Diaspora did not identify the incidence of sexual abuse immediately after the war. The Holocaust was so traumatic for Jews that it was not until many years afterwards that Survivors were able to discuss the topic and other people were able to listen. Another reason for this may be that therapists treating Holocaust Survivors might not have comprehended the true significance of what was being said, because they considered these experiences as part of an overall composite of atrocities suffered by these individuals. Other therapists, who are themselves second-generation Holocaust survivors, may avoid probing questions about the Survivor's possible sexual abuse because they fear what may be discovered. Danieli (1985), a therapist who works with the children of Holocaust Survivors, raised the possibility that these individuals did not question their parents about sexual abuse because they feared finding out that their mothers may have been raped.

Recent research has begun to address this subject. On the basis of information found in diaries and written testimonies, clinicians reported that Jewish women were terrorized by rape during the Holocaust. The fear of sexual assault was experienced by women in hiding. Lynton (1998) and Lev-Wiesel and Amir (2005) discussed sexually humiliating experiences in the concentration camps. For instance, both men and women of all ages were forced to undress and their genitals were shaved in public (Bitton & Jackson, 1980). Women and men had no privacy, in any respect, whatsoever.

One of the questions that arise in this context is: what happened to young adolescents and children? As we know, sexual terrorization at a young age is particularly traumatic (Finkelhor, 1990). A study conducted by Valent (1995), a researcher and clinician as well as a child Survivor himself, used the following variables to compare Holocaust child Survivors to adults who were sexually abused during childhood: psychological symptoms of distress, interpersonal relations, type of abuse experienced, coping skills and resilience. Valent's findings indicated that as adults, both child Holocaust Survivors and sexually abused children retrospectively reported similar trauma responses both at the time the trauma occurred and throughout their lives. Holocaust atrocities and childhood sexual abuse are considered by clinicians to be two of the most serious childhood traumas (Lev-Wiesel & Amir, 2005). Thus, the effects of the synergism of these factors would be expected to be particularly detrimental.

Though the real prevalence of sexual abuse among Holocaust Survivors remains unknown, children are always considered to be at high risk for sexual abuse during wartime. Systematic rape and other forms of sexual abuse of women and girls have been reported in many war zones around the world. In Bosnia, Herzegovina, Burundi, Sierra Leone and Northern Uganda, systematic rape, "forced marriages," and other forms of sexual abuse were and still are used as a weapon of war. Amone-P'Olak (2005), for example, who studied female child sexual abuse in Northern Uganda during the violent conflict between government forces and rebels, reported that over 26,000 children were abducted. Many were used as child soldiers and were physically and sexually abused while in rebel captivity (Amnesty International, 2004; Amone-P'Olak, 2003; Human Rights Watch, 1997, 2003; UNICEF, 1998).

In light of the research showing that victims of childhood sexual abuse tend not to discuss these issues directly in therapy or otherwise, it is especially likely that Holocaust Survivors who had experienced such trauma would not independently volunteer information. One study (Lev-Wiesel and Amir, 2005) explored the impact of childhood sexual abuse among multiple extreme traumas in Holocaust child Survivors. Twenty-two child Survivors of the Holocaust who were sexually abused during the war completed open-ended interviews that were qualitatively analyzed. Three major themes were found.

The first theme concerned issues relating to the sexual abuse trauma. Most participants described the sexual abuse events in detail and with coherence in relation to chronological time, age, circumstances, and content (for example, when it began, how old they were, what exactly happened, who the perpetrator was, what their own responses were, and so on). An interesting distinction was made by the Survivors between their past and current lives with regard to their symptoms. They reported that during the time of the abuse (usually during the war and its aftermath), they felt fear, horror, physical and emotional pain, and profound loneliness. However, years after the abuse, they reported symptoms of anxiety, numbness, emptiness, or depression. Although fear and horror haunt them at night in the form of nightmares, feelings of sadness and emptiness envelop them during the day.

The second theme concerned the survivors' perceptions of the reasons and explanations for the sexual abuse itself and for the behavior of the perpetrator. Being sexually abused (whether by Jewish or non-Jewish strangers, biological parents, or caretakers) was perceived as part of the targeted massive barbarity directed against them as Jews. Some even thought that they deserved the abuse, both physical and sexual, because of their Jewish origin (that it was somehow God's punishment for having been born a Jew or for Jews allegedly having murdered Jesus). Some explained that the perpetrators used abuse as a means of "educating" the Jews about their suitable social status. They, the Jewish children, were expected to serve and satisfy their "saviors" in any way they could. Although children were taught that Judaism was a source of evil, they simultaneously longed for their lost Jewish parents and thus, their heritage. This contradiction left them confused and frightened of their own feelings and beliefs.

A distinction was found between survivors' feelings toward Jewish and non-Jewish perpetrators. Survivors expressed clear negative feelings such as hatred, hostility, and disgust toward perpetrators who were Jews, particularly if they were their biological parents. Jewish children expected other Jews to help them, to be on their side, and to empathize with their fear and suffering. When Jews (apparently in relatively rare cases) were the actual perpetrators, the children learned that they were absolutely alone and could not trust anyone. Jewish perpetrators proved that the Gentile claim that Jews were evil was somehow correct, and the children could hate them with certainty. On the other hand, the Survivors expressed ambivalent feelings such as hate and love, resentment and longing, gratitude and anger toward perpetrators who were Christians, whether they were their "foster parents" or not. In the children's minds, these Gentile perpetrators did not have to save them, and yet they did so. Thus, besides having negative feelings, they also had feelings of thankfulness toward their saviors.

The third theme was the survivors' general valuation of their own lives. Despite the survivors' many achievements, including raising functional families and succeeding in business or careers, they were continually tortured by painful memories of their sexual abuse trauma. They reported being engaged in endless internal struggles to control anger, aggressiveness, or panic. Often their substantial difficulties in achieving intimacy with their spouses and children led them to find life meaningless and painful.

Telling these untold stories is important to the remaining Survivors as well as to future generations. According to Bar-Tur & Levy-Shiff (1994), as the Holocaust child Survivors enter their seventh and eighth decades, their main developmental task is to review their lives and construct a retrospective life story that is coherent and meaningful and helps them to cope with the daily obstacles of aging. In recent years, we have witnessed that Holocaust child Survivors shared their personal stories in diverse ways. Disclosure of deep emotional experiences and relaying one's traumatic story can have a therapeutic impact on personal well-being (Krell, 1993; Peenebaker, 1989; Peenebaker & Chung, 2007) and physical health (Peenebaker, 1989). Testimony presents the Survivor with an opportunity for self-expression and empowerment and as a result it might improve the Survivor's damaged self (Greenwald & Al, 2006).

For Holocaust child Survivors, remembering their survival story is also essential in passing on their family history. In a Holocaust child Survivor's family, future generations are often not only expected to remember and commit to retelling the Survivor's story, but to also pass on this obligation to those yet to come (Lev-Wiesel, 2007).

MARINA

I only saw my older brother occasionally because he studied in an out-of-town yeshiva. He was 13 years older than me, and our sister was about halfway between us in age. I was born in 1931, the youngest child of our father, a rabbi, and our mother, a merchant and manufacturer of religious clothing for Jewish women (such as hats and dresses with long skirts and long sleeves). Our mother traveled all over Europe buying and selling. She also established a factory and retail shops in her home country. Our father worked part-time in one of these shops, and he also devoted many hours to caring for me. He told me stories, discussed the Bible with me, and shared details about the lives of our ancestors. I prayed with my father, and we often went for long walks in the city. He was warm and personable, and I loved him very much. Our extended close family lived in various cities and towns, and I visited and vacationed with our relatives regularly. When I was little, I looked forward to staying at the homes of these welcoming aunts and uncles and our many playful cousins, even when my parents couldn't join me.

My life began to crumble when I was 8 years old. It was then that the Germans annexed my country of birth, Czechoslovakia. My parents welcomed a young woman into our home who had escaped Poland after its annexation by Germany. They gave her a part-time job in their factory. I grew close to our adopted guest, who told me much about what was happening in Poland. My parents expected that the injustices in Poland would be short lived. But it wasn't more than a few months before the Germans overtook Czechoslovakia.

My mother reasoned that because I was afforded such a rich religious life within our family, attending public school would help me to also be part of the larger society. I was a very enthusiastic student and made many Jewish and non-Jewish friends during elementary school. One day, the Germans abruptly demanded that the Jewish students study in classrooms separate from Christian students. At first, my teachers tried to keep me in the class because they liked me very much. But the authorities allowed no exceptions, and I, too, was segregated into a class with only Jewish students. I remember running out of my school and down the street, quickly searching for my father when I knew he would be walking to the synagogue. I was afraid that in his easily identifiable religious clothing with the required yellow star on his outer coat, he would be a target for beatings.

Just as my security and happiness in school was ending, my parents were stripped of their livelihoods. Government authorities commanded them to hand over their stores and factory to Christians by signing contracts stating that they did so of their own free will without expecting any payment. The officials told my parents that they would confiscate their properties regardless of consent, but if they didn't turn them over willingly, they would be executed, along with us children.

My mother tried to convince my father to flee the country. At first he resisted, and by the time he agreed, it was too late. He hadn't believed that our situation would get worse, and he thought that there would be an end to the persecutory discrimination we suffered. My mother and father couldn't find other jobs and started to live off of savings. My mother showed me where she hid the money in the garden.

During this time, my cousin, along with her husband and their two baby daughters, escaped from another city and knocked on our door asking to be hidden. I had spent vacations with this older cousin, and I loved her very much. She was devastated when my parents, out of fear, sent her and her husband and babies away after just one night. The Jews were warned that if they helped other Jews, as they often did, they would be executed. Even though I understood that it was too dangerous and that my parents were trying to protect us, I resented them for this decision, especially my mother. It was easier for me to primarily blame my mother, who was a resourceful, creative, independent person whom I resented for having been away from home so much, rather than my father, with whom I felt so close and had spent so much more time.

Several weeks after the German occupation, just a few days before Passover, our family received a flier declaring that Jews must leave their homes and should only pack a few things to take with them. The flier stated we would be relocated in a ghetto for Jews, provided work, and treated well. All five members of our immediate family walked out of our home, each carrying one small suitcase. My mother hid all her jewelry inside her shoes. The soldiers and police led us and the other Jews to a clearing in a huge forest outside of town. We all lived at this site for a month, without shelter, not even tents, and with only one meal a day. The men left every day to work—laying railroad tracks, loading and unloading rail cars, and building railroad stations. Little did they know that they were building the transportation system designed to destroy our people.

I don't remember this experience as a terrible one, but rather as though we were camping out. Even though I knew we were in danger, I stayed focused on the present. I was with my parents, and my father continued to tell me encouraging, engrossing, reassuring stories. As long as I was with my father, I felt protected and safe. I also had my Jewish friends for company. I remember watching a favorite teacher of mine who was pregnant and had her husband and toddler with her. I loved to watch how my teacher and her husband acted so lovingly toward each other and their baby. I was glad to be helping my teacher care for her little one.

An abrupt change came on the day we were packed into a cattle car of a train for eight hours. Many people were crowded together; it was very hot and we couldn't get enough air. We cried and shouted for help. Some people in the car vomited and died. No one knew where we were being taken. I sat on my father's lap. My father put his hands on my head and gave me his blessing. Then he said to me, "No matter what happens, you should always remember that you were very much loved and that I will go with you wherever you go, always."

The sliding doors of our rail car opened in a small town about 45 minutes from Auschwitz. When we arrived I sensed danger. I looked at the people on the platform—so skinny, like walking skeletons. The Germans administered the camp, but the guards were Lithuanians and Ukrainians who wore Nazi uniforms. They separated the men from the women. I was separated from my father and my friends but was still with my mother and sister. I could see my father and brother through the fence that separated men from women. My mother, my sister, and I walked several times a day to see my father and brother through the fence. Seeing my father even in this limited way still gave me some sense of protection.

I noticed that a Ukrainian guard often stared at me, and I felt uncomfortable being the target of his gaze. I was eleven years old and had long blonde hair, green eyes, and a child's body that hadn't yet reached puberty. One day he called me over and took me into his cabin, closed the door, and started to talk to me. I felt that he was talking nicely to me but sensed that there was something else behind his words. I didn't fully understand what he was saying because we didn't speak the same language fluently. He stroked my hair, and I understood that he said things like, "You are a nice girl. If you need something ask me, and I will take care of you. I will be sure to take care of your parents, too."

The first time the guard let me go after talking to me. I didn't tell anyone what had happened because I didn't know how or what to say. The guard kept making advances. He brought me to his cabin, where he started to stroke my hair, putting his hands on different parts of my body, and moving his fingers under my shirt. I couldn't move because I was too frightened and didn't know how to get out of this situation. I had no one to tell. I didn't want to worry my mother, who was weak from diarrhea and dehydration, and I instinctively knew that no one could help me. It wasn't long before we heard that we would be sent to Auschwitz. I remember being partially relieved because I wanted to get out of the situation I found myself in at the camp.

When we arrived at Auschwitz, our family was able to gather together at the gate. The guard who had molested me was there too. He came up to me and told me not to worry because he would take care of us. New arrivals were summarily divided up, one side for women and one side for men. There was no fence—we just stood apart and could see each other. We were immediately forced to undress in public, and we were shaved of all hair on our heads and genitals. I remember how awful it was to undress in front of everyone, to have my genital hair shaved, and to lose my long hair that I loved. Then I was tattooed by being branded with a number on my arm. I pushed the pain aside by thinking about how much I wanted to be with my father. I always searched for him and wanted to be with him, and nothing else mattered to me in comparison. We Jews were divided into two lines. I understood that those in one line will go to Birkenau, and those in the other will go to the crematorium.

I was very young and not tall for my age; usually the Nazis did not let Jewish children like me live. But the guard who had abused me was there and made sure that I was sent to the left. All of my family, with the exception of my brother, was forced to the right. My sister, seven years older than me, and our mother and father were pushed to the crematorium. My teacher, who had tried to speak with her husband through the fence before arriving at Auschwitz, was now in line with him, their toddler, and their newborn baby. All were marching to their death. That was the end of my beloved teacher and her family and the image of marital and family love they represented. From the moment I saw my father selected to go to the other side, I completely and permanently forgot how to speak Czech, my first language. I obliterated it so completely from my memory that, even up until today, when I hear Czech spoken, I can't identify it.

Afterward, I relied solely on my second language, Hungarian, to talk with the teenagers who took me under their wing in Birkenau. Birkenau was a death camp, but the guards put the inmates to work daily until they ordered their killing. The older kids thought of me as a younger sister and formed a kind of a family that took care of me. I had become numb and completely emotionally detached when the guards took my father away. I was indifferent to the hunger, cold, humiliation, and torture and didn't care whether I lived or died. I didn't care if I ate or how cold I felt. The teenagers placed me between themselves at night so their body heat would keep me warmer, and they told me when to eat my meager rations. I acted like a robot and did what I was told.

At the end of the war, a friend and I went back to our home city. Representatives from an organization in Israel were searching for orphaned Jewish children to give them safe passage to Israel. They brought us children together and told us about Israel and about reestablishing a country for the Jews. They trained us child Survivors in how to immigrate illegally to Israel—when to be quiet, when and how to fight. Overtime the spirit of group obligation and support grew among us. I remember this as a positive time period, when I started to feel some emotion again. The other kids and I were sharing some positive experiences, hope and excitement about arriving in a place that would be ours and where we would be safe.

While preparing for Aliyah (the emigration of Jews to Israel), I had hoped that some of my relatives who were then in Canada and the United States and whom I used to visit as a child in Czechoslovakia, would invite me to come to live with them. I wrote and asked them to take me, and they answered that I would be better off with my friends and that I should emigrate to Israel. It took me years to forgive them because I just couldn't understand how they could have refused to help me.

After a year in this youth movement, we were sent on a ship to Israel. The English stopped the ship at sea and diverted it to Cyprus, where we spent several months before being permitted to leave. When we finally arrived in Israel, my friends and I who were from religious families were sent to a religious village in which every family "adopted" one or two adolescents. It was a terrible time. I, like the other teens, couldn't readapt to family life. I couldn't stand to watch families being together, because it reminded me of my own family. The pain was too much. We couldn't stay there; we just wanted out. Finally, the leaders understood and sent all us kids to an agricultural boarding high school.

We lived together, speaking Hungarian as we continued to learn Hebrew. We, child Survivors, didn't want to talk about our losses or our past experiences. We only wanted to talk about the future and what had to be done to establish the State of Israel.

When the war for Israel's independence started, my friends and I were sent to a kibbutz, to guard the border. After the war, my future husband and I met on a trip in Israel. I had long blond hair again; he was tall and handsome, also a child Survivor and we fell in love. My husband took care of me in ways similar to those of my father. I was often scared to leave the house. Whenever I was at a train station or in places crowded with many people, I would feel terrified and fainted. My husband made it possible for me to stay home and not have to work outside the house as he took care of all my basic needs. I felt capable of taking care of things in our home, doing all kinds of needlework, cooking, and baking.

On our first anniversary, I gave birth to our eldest daughter. Four years later, we had a second daughter. Having my daughters meant everything to me. They gave me life again; I could live. I felt that I had triumphed; the fact that my daughters were alive showed that my husband and I had beaten the Nazis. I played with our girls and told them stories, nurturing them as my father had done for me. We made dolls together and they put on puppet shows. I told them about their grandfather and my joyous childhood vacations, concentrating on memories before the Holocaust and rarely mentioning what the war had been like for us. When I needed to go outside, I would take my daughters with me and hold their hands as tight as I could. I felt as though nothing could happen to me as long as I maintained my grasp on my girls. Taking care of our daughters shed some of my fears away. I brought this same intensity to my relationship with our grandchildren, often sitting for hours building Lego skyscrapers with our grandsons and taking them to amusement parks.

The way I felt about our children and grandchildren quelled some of my fears, but I could not stop feeling depressed, and I was still afraid to go out and would feel faint when I did. I was diagnosed as having epilepsy and given medicines that not only didn't help me, but brought on other complications and made me feel worse. One day I threw out all the drugs, because I knew what worked for me better than my doctors did. Now I know that my illness was not epilepsy, but post-traumatic stress disorder.

My cousin who had stayed with our family for that one single night had managed to escape to Canada and then immigrated to Israel. My cousin's family kept in touch with me and we were close over the years. But my relationship with my brother was minimal up until the time of his death. He lived in New York, and became extremely religious. Though we hardly knew each other as children and followed such different paths as adults, in order to let me know that he thought of me my brother sent me loving letters and gifts such as a Kiddush cup.

After I was diagnosed with cancer, I asked my older daughter to accompany me on a trip to Auschwitz, where I had seen my parents and sister for the last time. Before traveling to the concentration camp, I stopped off in my hometown and I told my daughter that I needed to come back here to find the little girl that I had lost. All these many years later, I was still scared of the people around us and while traveling on the commuter train to Auschwitz, I forbade my daughter from speaking to me in Hebrew. As soon as I entered the camp grounds, I walked straight to the crematorium holding the 21 candles I brought. Inside that dark, frightening space, I began lighting each candle in the name of our family members, my beloved teacher, and two other members of my teacher's family. The last candle I lit on behalf of the Jewish people. After I had lit all the candles, I remember collapsing and screaming at my father's memory: How could you leave me? You promised not to leave me! Why didn't you take me with you? I was screaming as the eleven-year-old girl I had been.

After a seemingly endless time in the crematorium that was probably only about 15 minutes, we left to return to Israel. As we were leaving, I remembered what my grandson had told me before we left: "Remember as you go to meet your 'parents,' that you have a family here that loves you; and I love you and I want you to come back to me." His words reminded me of what my father had told me on the train to Auschwitz: that he would always love me and be there for me.

DAVID

I was born in Northern France on May 30, 1930. My brother was six years older than me. Shortly after I was born, our parents moved to Gent, Belgium, hoping our father's skill in jewelry designing would bring a higher salary there. We were living in Gent when the Nazis invaded. I don't remember my mother, who died of tuberculosis when I was four. I was a frail child who spent much of his early years in children's health facilities at the seashore. When my father remarried in 1937, I was finally taken home to enjoy a more ordinary family life. Because of this, I consider my stepmother to be my mother. I attended public school in Gent and spent summer vacations at children's camps in the woods. I don't remember more than this about my childhood during the prewar period. Perhaps I blocked out the memories of a protected childhood because they would have been far too painful to remember during my time in hiding.

On a Thursday in the Spring of 1940, I awoke to the sounds of German warplanes bombing our city. I ran to my parents' bed shouting, "The Germans are here!" My father listened to the Nazi speeches broadcast over the radio and told my brother, who was 16 at the time, to pack up and try to book passage to England so he could continue his studies. A few days after waving goodbye to my brother at the Grand Central Station in Antwerp, my father decided that we should all go to England immediately. We packed up and returned to the Grand Central Station. We stood in line for almost a whole day to purchase tickets and then, finally, we boarded the train. The 49 kilometer ride from Gent to Brussels took us four days. Each time the German planes attacked the rail lines, the train stopped. By the time we arrived in Brussels, Belgium had already capitulated to the Germans. The borders were closed, necessitating our return to Gent, where we lived in a comfortable apartment. My brother also returned because he never made it out of the country.

The tenants living downstairs belonged to the National Socialist Movement and called us dirty Jews at every opportunity. My father moved us into a rented apartment in a Jewish neighborhood, where we lived for about a year and a half. I attended a public school because at first the school authorities did not know I was a Jew. After a while, the kids realized I was Jewish and began taunting me with verbal obscenities. To spare me this harassment, my father transferred me to a Jewish school. After a short time, I noticed that some children stopped coming to school altogether. I asked my father what was happening to my schoolmates. He said, "They have probably moved to England."

In 1942 an order was issued for Jews to sew a yellow Star of David onto their outer clothing. Soon after, my father was not allowed to work as a jewelry designer. I began to go out and steal food and wood for heating. My brother, who was 18, was sent to a facility for undernourished teenage boys in Tielt, Belgium. In May 1942, my father received a telegram from the German authorities ordering him to pack his clothes and report to the Grand Central Station on Saturday morning at 10:00 o'clock. Of course, my parents knew what was happening, but I didn't know; I was only 12 years old. My mother cried, "Don't go, love; don't go, don't go." She was hanging onto his coat, pleading, "Don't leave me." My father kissed my mother and me goodbye and left. We never saw him again. He was killed in Auschwitz on November 18, 1942.

I continued to attend school, and once again, that summer my mother sent me to a health camp for children. Only a few days after my return home, I heard pounding on the front door at around 4 a.m. We opened the door and the Gestapo and Belgian police barged in, ordering us to get out of the house immediately. My mother already had the suitcases packed because she anticipated something like this. Trucks lined the street. It was still dark outside. They were rounding up all the Jews on the street. They were so efficient . . . . They put the people in the trucks in alphabetical order. I was in the last truck.

The truck started to roll very slowly. My mother told me to jump. I was crying. She said, "You know you have to jump." She pushed me, so I jumped out of the truck and ran and ran. I had no idea where to go. I was walking the streets for a couple of hours wondering where my mother and neighbors had been taken. I asked some people where the trucks were going and discovered that the Germans were assembling the Jews at a school at the far side of town. It was daylight by the time I walked all the way to that school. German soldiers guarded the school, but I sneaked inside to find my mother. She was sitting on her suitcase crying. When she saw me she was furious. She said, "I don't want to see you. Get out of here." I was crying as I slinked out past a German guard. My mother was killed in Auschwitz in December 1942.

I went to the home of some Christian friends of my parents. They took me in but told me up front, "You cannot stay here; it's too dangerous." They contacted an underground organization called the White Brigade, which made contact with my brother, who was still in the sanatorium. They brought me to the director of the sanatorium, John Boudewijn. This sanatorium and a second sanatorium, just 29 kilometers away, where my brother subsequently hid, were both supported by the Belgium government. The Germans never came inside sanatoriums because they were afraid of contracting diseases.

Nevertheless, word got around in the city where my brother was living that there was a Jew in town, and that was considered dangerous. Through the mail, my brother was ordered to leave the sanatorium, and he was eventually shipped to Auschwitz. Director John approached me and warned, "It would be best if you were baptized as a Catholic." My being able to remain at the sanatorium was conditional upon this conversion. A priest who worked there taught me about Catholicism and in 1943, I was baptized Catholic.

Soon after my conversion to Catholicism, John informed me, "Listen, it's getting too dangerous for you to stay here. You are going to have to come and live with me and my family. The Germans may come inside to look for you."

After a year of living in the sanitarium, I went to live with his family. And they, well . . . it's very difficult to talk about my time in John's home.

Soon after I had moved in, I was sitting in a tree in their huge backyard picking cherries. Next door, there was an enormous commotion; the Gestapo was searching all over the neighbor's backyard. They were looking for me but they had the wrong address, number 35 instead of 37. So it was relatively safe for me to stay there for a long time—in terms of protection from the Gestapo.

The Boudewijns had seven children but used me to do all the chores in the house. I chopped wood several times every day for the stove. I washed dishes, did laundry, peeled potatoes, polished shoes, scrubbed the floors on all three levels of the house, and emptied each child's urine pans.

A private Catholic school approached me with a scholarship. The scholarship was in John's honor because he saved a Jew through conversion—me. He even made me knock on all the neighbors' doors to introduce myself as "the Jewish child" that John brought into the Catholic fold. But within his home, John's children constantly heckled me as a dirty Jew. Every night, I went to bed crying. Sometimes I went to John in tears, and he would slap me in the face. Many times John told me that my parents and I were being punished because the Jews had crucified Christ. He said that as Jews we were doomed for eternity.

If I did something wrong, John would beat me with his shoes. He would strike me with his hands over the smallest blunders. He would beat me with anything he could find. He would use any excuse to punish me and to send me to bed without supper. One time, his son told him I was laughing in the attic where I slept. He called me downstairs and punched me until my eyes were all swollen. One of my problems was that I wet my bed until age 14. He beat me every time I wet my bed. He took the mattress and replaced it with wood. From that time on, I was forced into sleeping naked on the wood in the attic throughout all the years that I lived with the Boudewijns.

Another time one of John's sons hammered nails into a bench and told his father that I had done it. John had me put my hands on the kitchen sink so that he could thrash my knuckles and fingers with a stick. He hit me so hard and for so long that even his wife pleaded with him to stop. Sometimes he would force me to kneel on my wooden shoes. My knees would be inside my shoes and I had to remain kneeling for an hour or two. Whenever something went wrong in the family, someone would cry "David did it, David did it." John would come to me and I would say, "No, I didn't do it." He would insist, "Yes, you did," and I'd maintain, "No, I didn't do it," and he'd begin to slap me silly. I would never admit to something I didn't do. It also made him furious when I wasn't crying. He was a big man, and he was left handed. He hit me on my right side until I cried. I completely lost my hearing in my right ear and still have an extremely weak right eye.

Confusingly, John would sometimes be nice to me. On those occasions he'd come to me, put his hands on my head, kiss me, and say "I like you; you are a very nice boy." The very next day his behavior toward me would be the exact opposite.

I sang in the church choir because I had a clear soprano voice. The people at church thought I was John's son, so this made him feel proud—that was his son singing up there. Sometimes, when he sat in the living room, he'd shout for me to come and sing for him. One time, his wife heard me when I was singing on demand and thought I was goofing off instead of doing my chores. She came up behind me with a huge milk container and smashed it on my head. John jumped out of his chair and pounded her in front of me. He told me to come back and sing for him. Of course I was too frightened to be able to sing, so he sent me to my room for the whole day without food.

That was the night that John came to my room for the first time and took off my underwear. He said that he never saw a circumcised boy, so he wanted to see "it." After that night, he came to my room repeatedly and would check me out and fondle me.

John had a daughter who was 13, one year younger than me at the time. Every Friday night he would fill a tin tub with hot water and put me and his daughter in the tub together. He would just stand there and watch to see whether I would get an erection. I never did get an erection, but I wonder what he would have done if I had.

John's wife was a heavyset woman. Whenever I was occupied with chores in the kitchen, she would enter and begin sweeping the floor with her hands. She would bend over wearing a short skirt with no underwear right in front of me.

So many things happened to me when I was living with that family, but there are many things I don't remember to this day . . . .

I had few personal belongings. My mother had thrown a postcard out of the train. She had written on it, "Whoever finds this, please mail this." She had addressed it to her friends. She thought I would be there, but of course I wasn't; however, they sent the postcard to the sanatorium. John's children found the postcard and they tore it up. I had a harmonica that my father had given me for my birthday. I was quite musical and I loved to play the harmonica. The children stole it and buried it in the backyard. The last present my father gave me was a book, and one day I found all the pages torn from it.

John thought I should study at a seminary to become a Jesuit priest. He said it was his reward for all that he had done for me. I loved the seminary, and for two years earned straight A's. But John insisted that I write to him every other day and inform him about the details of my life. He used this information to find fault with the family with whom I lived. He concluded that the Russian wife of that family must be a communist and that her husband was the Antichrist because he didn't go to church every Sunday. The end result was that John recalled me to his home and prevented me from returning to the seminary. He said, "I think you're old enough now that you should help us financially." I got a job in a bakery, making bread on the night shift and delivering it on a bicycle in the morning. He made me quit that job so I could return home and resume my former chores. As before, I chopped wood, cleaned the house, and did everything else, even mended socks and ironing. I was treated like garbage. Eventually John stopped insisting that I get in the tub with his daughter.

There was an organization in Belgium that gave special benefits and public recognition to people with large families. They hosted celebrations to honor women who had seven or more children. They also brought a filmmaker to the town to document this event. The Boudewijn family was a recipient of these benefits and media attention. John sent me to wait for the photographer at the bus station and accompany him to his destination. The photographer asked me to come the next day to help him. He told me that he needed an assistant and would teach me all about photography and film development. I was very interested but needed to check with John before I could agree to his offer. John gave his approval on condition that all the money I earned be handed directly to him.

In 1945 my brother returned from Germany with tuberculosis. He was transferred to a sanatorium near Huy for treatment. I didn't know what he had gone through during the war years, nor did I share my experiences with him. One day John received an urgent cable asking him to come to the sanatorium immediately. They expelled my brother because he had seduced a nun who consequently renounced her vows. John told my brother never to return and forbade me from ever speaking with him again. He tore up all the pictures I had of my brother, claiming, "If this is what the Jews do, they deserve everything that happens to them."

For the next four years, I didn't see or hear from my brother. In May 1949, when I was 19, John declared, "The Pig [his name for my brother] found that you have an uncle who survived the war and lives in France. The Pig wants to go to live with your uncle and to meet you to say goodbye. Write your brother and tell him you never want to see him again." I did so, but my brother didn't buy it and insisted that I meet him. John consented to letting me see my brother only after I did excessive amounts of chores. When I met my brother, he asked if I wanted to return with him to our uncle's. I cried and wanted to go, but I was scared to death to ask John for permission.

During the entire period in John's home, I only fought back once. The incident took place two weeks before I saw my brother again, when Mrs. Boudewijn threatened to throw a big rock at me for not completing a chore adequately. I lifted a shovel and dared her to go ahead and throw the stone. Thus, it took much courage for me to confront John about my wish to join my brother. When I did, he became enraged, throwing me out of the house, shouting, "You came here with nothing and you are going to leave this house with nothing." I left for France immediately, at 5 a.m. that day.

My uncle demanded that my brother and I pay him for our stay and buy flowers regularly for his wife. In December, my brother returned to Belgium and I was left alone. One night my uncle and aunt went to the movies and I wrote my brother complaining about my uncle. My uncle found the letter and threw me out of the house. They had a maid, Elizabeth, and with her I was with a woman for the first time. I loved her. When she found out that I had been thrown out of the house, she arranged for me to stay at her parents' place.

I enlisted in the Belgian Air Force as a photographer. Those were the best two years of my life. After I was discharged, I freelanced as a photographer and managed a camera store. Elizabeth worked as a stewardess. In 1954 she became pregnant, so we married. Elizabeth had a rough pregnancy and died in childbirth; our son was born prematurely but survived. At the time of my wife's death, my uncle and aunt wrote and offered their help. I didn't hear back from my brother after I sent him a message about my wife's death, nor did he come to my wife's funeral. After several weeks, my son was released from the hospital, and I found some friends who could care for him while I worked at the camera shop.

One day at the shop I felt someone's eyes on me. I turned around to find my brother staring at me. I was furious. Some years previously, he had contacted me after he learned that my father had had a life insurance policy and that we might receive a settlement. He asked if I could give him my portion because he was getting married and needed the money. I consented, but then the process took several years, after which I also needed funds. My brother was infuriated that I had changed my mind. I never saw any of the money, and I was still angry that he had ignored my wife's death. We made peace that day, but subsequently lost all contact after his third marriage, when he changed his name to a Christian-sounding one. I imagine that he tried to cut himself off from the horrors of the past. In so doing, he had to dissociate himself from me, of course, because I was a constant reminder of his previous life.

A cousin who lived in the United States contacted me in 1955 and asked if I wanted to emigrate. It took me a year to obtain a visa and leave Belgium. I worked in a camera store in Portland, Oregon. Later, I became a partner in a camera shop and then its sole owner. Financially, I was successful.

I married a fellow immigrant from Belgium, but the marriage ended soon after I discovered that she was beating my son while I was at work. In 1968, I fell in love with Josephine, to whom I have been married for 35 years. She is a warm, smart, giving person who worked as a lawyer protecting women's rights. We had two daughters and now have four grandchildren. I didn't know how to build relationships with my children, so I was a distant father. I am a better grandfather than I was a father, but I still do not know how to relate to children. My son graduated from a military academy with honors and enlisted in the U.S. Air Force. In 1980, just two weeks after his marriage, he and his bride were killed in a car accident.

My wounds from the war remain open. To this day, whenever I see a police car, I drive to the side of the road and stop because I still get so anxious. Emotionally, on some level, I believe that the police are coming after me to do me harm. I cannot speak about my life in those days even in factual, intellectualized terms. The very first time I told part of my story was when I was interviewed by the Spielberg Foundation.

While I lived with them, I called John and his wife mama and papa. If John were alive today, I wouldn't even talk to him; however, I did attend his funeral. Once I got a letter from John asking me to recommend him to Yad Vashem so he could be honored as a "Righteous Gentile." (Yad Vashem, a memorial, was established in Jerusalem in 1953 to commemorate the 6 million Jewish victims of the Holocaust.) Compliantly, I wrote the letter, but fortunately, he didn't receive the status.

With all the abuse he perpetrated against me, John still saved my life. Yet, that act has remained a double-edged sword for me. Even as fortunate as I have been in the years since the war, I still believe that my life isn't worth living. Every night before I close my eyes, I pray to God that I won't see the morning. My daily prayer has gone unanswered all these years.

CONDOLISA

The most horrible event, the one that deeply hurt me, was when they arrested my father. That was the first blow. I was six years old when my father was seized by the French police. Even though I had heard that Jews were being arrested in the streets, I still felt safe with my father, mother and baby brother together in our one-room apartment. My parents shielded us. I felt I was allowed to still be a child. I had no responsibilities.

The first time my father was kidnapped was when he had gone to the market. Sometimes, in order to arrest large number of Jews, police trucks entered from both sides of a road and demanded that the people trapped there show their identity cards. During one such raid, they snatched my father. I was very attached to him, and his disappearance was devastating. I kept asking my mother when Pa would be back. Then, one day, I had a premonition of my father's return. I was very excited all day; I couldn't sit still. I told my mother that Pa would return that day. My mother became angry and told me not to torture myself thinking that my father would return at any moment and that if he came, I would see him. But then, from our apartment on the third floor, I heard his familiar footsteps outside in the street. My mother told me that I was talking nonsense. I remember having a vivid imagination and being very sensitive to sounds, voices, and smells. I was one hundred percent certain it was my father's footsteps that I heard on the street, and sure enough, they were.

He entered our apartment accompanied by the baker's wife. She had been thrilled when she saw him through the bakery window, and she rushed outside to give him some bread and usher him home. I jumped into my father's lap, which was my beloved usual place to listen to his many stories. At this time he told my mother, the baker's wife and me that he had been held in a camp in Paris during November 1941. He noticed that if detainees got sick, they were released. He had some kind of dysentery and was given pills that he didn't swallow. So he was allowed out of the camp. I think that this was great luck, because later on the sick were the first to be sent to the concentration camps.

One night in July 1942, a thousand Jews were arrested. The police carried out a surprise attack, seizing men, women, and children from their beds and rushing them out of their homes. The police targeted specific houses and apartments because they had a list of names and addresses from residential registration information supplied by the municipality. Among those kidnapped were my maternal aunt and all of my cousins, even the babies. During that night, my aunt's husband was not at home. He had been searching for housing in the so-called "free zone" outside of Paris, which he considered to be safer for his family, only to return and not find them.

My father was at work, when my mother heard that if she would promise to support her sister and her daughters she would be able to obtain their release from incarceration. It was dangerous to do so, but she didn't waste any time. She immediately took me and my one-year-old brother to Paris on the train. I remember standing in a line for a long time before mother had the chance to talk to the authorities. I was choking, there was no air. When we arrived at the head of the line, my mother begged the man in charge to release her sister and the children, promising to assume full responsibility for them. When he unyieldingly refused, she asked the authorities to at least give her the children. They stiffly refused again; it had all been a deception. There was no choice—we returned home without them.

My father was arrested for the second time in 1943. They had all kinds of methods for expelling Jews. One such way was to force them out of their homes; another was to close off a street and snatch the people within the barricade. A third method, the one used this time to capture my father, was to order people to come to them under the ruse of checking their papers. During the war, there wasn't enough food, so coupons were distributed to the French population, based on age and how many coupons you could afford. Without coupons, there was no access to food. Jews received coupons marked "Jew." In order to receive the food necessary for survival, you had to show a coupon and thus, reveal that you were a Jew. It was through this exposure that my father was given a written pronouncement that he must go to the municipal authorities to check his ID papers.

I was six and a half in January of 1943, and I remember my parents arguing. My mother insisted, "Don't go; I know it is a trap. They want to keep you. If you go you won't come back." My mother wanted to show up at the authorities instead of my father. But he didn't agree. Nevertheless, when he was at work she took my father's papers to the authorities. They said that they didn't ask for her, but for him, and he had to be the one to appear. Now she knew for sure that he would be arrested. He didn't want to hear it. He was adamant. He said, "If I don't go they will take you and the children." I don't remember what I did or whether or not I tried to convince my father not to go. I recall this scene as if I am watching a play and am not there at all. My father decided to go.

I had gone to school that day and remember returning with this huge stone on my heart. I walked in the door at 4:30 in the afternoon. Usually, when I returned from school I would do all kinds of nonsense, but this time I didn't feel like it. I was very serious. I saw my mother in the middle of the room sitting bent over on a chair and I immediately asked her what happened to Pa. My mother said, "Pa's stubborn and they took him." I came over to her and put my head on her knees, and I cried. Then my mother told me, "I arranged it so that when you come back from school we will be able to go and say goodbye to Pa."

The two of us left right away. We entered the station and noticed policemen sitting about and saw my father behind bars with criminals. They allowed him out of the cell to return home and gather some clothing. But two French guards in uniform came home with us. On one side, my father held my hand, and on the other he held my mother's hand. The guards flanked us as we turned onto our street, and I became ashamed and embarrassed. There weren't many people walking in the street, but still I felt as if everyone was looking at us as though we were criminals. When we reached our place, my mother gave my father his best suit, the one he wore on Shabbat. She gave him bread and some money. At the last minute, my father remembered to take my baby tooth that had recently fallen out, and he told me that he would guard it. I can't remember if I even kissed him good-bye. All I know is that my tooth was lost in Auschwitz . . . I never saw my father again.

One month later, in February, my family received a scripted postcard from my father telling us that he was traveling to some place unknown to him. The German soldiers and their collaborators had such postcards that they required their captives to send. This postcard was among the things that my mother kept, but regretfully it disappeared. It was the last sign of life that remained of my father.

Life, somehow, went on without my father. My mother knew that the options for rescuing him were nonexistent. Before he was taken away my mother had begged him to approach his boss at the factory where he worked. She wasn't under any illusions that this boss cared a bit about Jews, but she knew that he hated the Germans, having lost his leg as a soldier during World War I. My mother tried to convince my father to ask his boss to help us find a place to hide. My father didn't want to. After the war, when my mother, brother, and I went to visit this man, he immediately asked after my father. When my mother admitted to him what she had wanted her husband to do, the man declared that my father had been a fool because he surely would have helped us. In hindsight, I think there is no way to know what would have happened. Many people who were initially hidden were later given up to the Germans. Before my father had been arrested for the second and last time, he had had a forewarning that he would be picked up. I wonder whether he accepted his fate and missed some chances of surviving because of this.

When my father was no longer at home, I began to sleep in the same bed with my mother. Our bed was next to the door. One night I dreamt two scenarios that appeared on both sides of a "screen" with a line down the middle. On one side of the screen, I was in a bright yellow room, and on the other side, I saw people standing in the dark. Suddenly the dream merged with reality. I heard people knocking on the door and whispered to my mother. My mother warned me to be quiet and not to answer. My brother was sleeping in his bed. Policemen under the guidance of a neighbor were behind the door. The neighbor shouted, "Mrs. P., open the door! We know you're home." The policemen threatened to break the door down. My mother didn't have a choice. The two policemen demanded to see our identity papers. My mother confronted them, shouting, "What! It's two o'clock in the morning; aren't you ashamed to come now and check papers?" After she presented them with our papers, they asked where her husband was and she had the courage to answer, "You already took care of it. You got him." Then they looked at my brother and asked if he was already 2 years old. Her mother defiantly said, "Look at the papers! Can't you read them?" The police said that this time my mother was lucky, but they told her they'd be back. There was a law that children under the age of two were not taken. This night raid in March of 1943 served as a warning signal to my mother, who rushed into action to secure hiding places for us.

By April, my mother had found a family to take care of us. She told me that I would have to go first and my brother would stay with her for a little while longer because he was a baby. She assured me that she, as the mother of the family, would be fine by herself. A teenage girl showed up at our place to take me. I had a small suitcase and a little bag with perfume bottles to which my mother had added water because they still exuded some scent. My mother also packed a makeup box with a picture on its cover that my father had given her and told me, "Keep it. It's from of your father, and if we meet after the war you will give it back to me. If not, it will be yours." I didn't cry when I said goodbye and left home. I hugged myself so I wouldn't cry. I suddenly became mature. Until they took my father away, I was a spoiled child. There wasn't anything I wanted that I didn't get. Sometimes my parents quarreled because my mother didn't want to give me something, but my father always wanted to.

I was only seven years old… The teenage girl took hold of my hand, and with my other hand I held onto my little bag as if it were gold. As we walked down the street a neighbor saw me and asked if I was leaving. I told her, "Yes, I have to." We rode the metro and arrived at a basement apartment with windows just above ground level. Walking into that apartment was hard for me. I was alone. With my mother I felt safe. I didn't have my father, but at least I had had my mother. This time, I was alone—no father, no mother, not even a little brother. I was among strangers; me, who never left home for anything, was among strangers.

My mother had told me to write to her, though she said that she wasn't sure if she would be able to answer. She told me that if I felt happy and well then I should write that. However, she warned me never to write if I wasn't being treated well or didn't feel well because if people found out they might harm me. My mother suggested that we have a secret symbol between us, and she knew that I loved to draw. She told me, "I want you to end every letter with a drawing. Draw a heart if you feel good. If you feel bad, draw a boat and I will know that you want to go away and leave that house." I didn't write to my mother very often and didn't receive many letters in return. Every time I wrote I ended the letter with a heart, except for one time.

Before I left home my mother had taken me to a hairdresser to get my hair cut. She explained to me that the people with whom I would be living might not have the patience to help me take care of my long hair. My mother assured me that she was going to save my hair for me. In spite of my mother's directness, preparation, and assurance, I found it hard to give up my hair. I felt half naked.

There were two other Jewish children in the basement apartment, one my age and one younger. The caretakers prepared the bed and designated a corner for me.

The minute that I went to bed and the lights were turned off, my world collapsed. Without my father, away from my mother, I wondered who these people were that I now depended on. I was afraid of the unknown, in addition to all my other fears. I cried quietly, not wanting anyone to hear me. Many times I would secretly cry at night and try to behave normally during the day. In the morning, after the first night in that basement, I ran to the window and could see some light because the shutters were not totally closed. I noticed a woman talking to a child and the image twisted my heart. I saw myself as that child and that woman as my mother. I went to school that morning, but I don't remember what I learned or what we did that day. My primary memory is standing in the school yard alone, not having friends and feeling lonely and apart from everyone.

About a month later, my caretakers told me that the same young woman who brought me to them would now pick up my brother and bring him over. This was great news for me. I went outside and waited for my little brother. I was so happy to see him walking toward me, calling me by my nickname. He was so cute with his fat belly. When my brother was born, I thought of him as if he was my real doll, and I learned how to care for him. Now, I felt that my responsibility was to be a mother to him. My brother and I didn't receive enough food. Our caretakers were not denying us, there just wasn't enough food in the house. In our own home, I hardly paid attention to food. My mother even had to remind me to eat. But now, I was always hungry. There was a woman who made visits to check on my brother and me as well as other Jewish children in different houses. One day she came and told me that she would be moving me and my brother to a different location.

As a transitional hiding place we were taken to a Jewish institution where we were among hundreds of children we didn't know. The first thing I remember is having my head shaved, as was done to the other children. I had the same embarrassed feeling that everyone was looking at me as I had had while walking down our street with my mother and father flanked by policemen. It was then as I stood frozen in humiliation that a boy came up to me, took my hand, said to me, "You can't stay like this," and coaxed me to come with him to the warehouse to find a hat. I'm amazed that though he was only ten, he had the insight to respond so sensitively to me when I was seven. He befriended me and looked after me, saying goodnight to me every night before he went up to the second floor where the kids in his age group slept. It haunts me that although I remember the names of many children who were at this institution, I can't remember any identifying information at all about this kind soul. I suspect he was murdered in Auschwitz.

After a couple of months, my brother and I moved in with our second family, and this one proved to be bad in every way. We lived with a mother and her 15-year-old son. I felt very, very bad there, and I was terrified of him. I became nervous and embarrassed when he would give me a dirty look. Even now, it's hard for me to talk about it. This teenage boy would come into my bed at night and force me to undress, touch his penis, do other things and keep quiet. I think that his mother knew what was going on and permitted it because she saw how he looked at me during the day. When I was washing in the bathroom, his mother sometimes came in and left the door open. She would even call him over to bring things to her or to ask him a question, giving her son a chance to see me naked. During this time I was really afraid that I would become pregnant, and then what would I do? Without accurate knowledge about sex, I worried that I would begin to menstruate and this would be the sign that I was pregnant. As I experienced these difficult things, I began to get use to seeing the world as dark and dangerous. I made myself think that only bad things would happen to me, because then if something good would happen, I would be surprised and happy. But if something bad happened, it wouldn't surprise me because I had expected it.

I sent my mother a letter that ended with a drawing of a ship. This was the only letter to my mother that survived the war years. My mother couldn't travel to visit us because it was too dangerous. But I knew that my mother had gotten the message and was afraid about what was happening to me because one of our former non-Jewish neighbors showed up at the house where we were staying. Her coming was such a pleasant surprise because I knew she was a goodhearted, sensitive, smart woman who loved me a lot. But I still didn't open up to her about the sexual abuse I was going through. I didn't tell her that it was horrible living there, but she saw it and she sensed my fear. I never told anyone what had happened to me in this family until six years ago. I began to experience insomnia, and after a battery of tests didn't detect a physical problem, I was referred to a psychologist. The psychologist recommended that I open up and talk about traumatic events during the Holocaust. That was the first time that I ever told anyone about what happened with that boy.

Several months after our former neighbor visited my brother and me, we were finally moved to another place that was very, very good. Unlike other children who never saw their parents again, I knew that my mother was somehow able to keep track of us. Later, I learned that my mother found this new family for us by soliciting the help of an acquaintance's granddaughter who had converted to Judaism but who worked for a minister.

This married couple had a 16-year-old son who, as a French soldier, had been arrested by the Germans. One chilly autumn day when I came home from school, the woman gave me a small sweater for my brother. It was on her son's teddy bear, and she exclaimed, "The bear doesn't need it." I took it right over to my brother, and it fit him. These were good people. I also adored the woman's husband, who gardened and patiently taught me about tending plants. He worked in a factory, and my mother was able to send me letters through him. My brother and I were fed good food and treated warmly; I felt safe as if we were living with our grandparents. Unfortunately, after just two months we had to be taken from this home because my brother and I had contracted a contagious skin disease.

We were transferred to our next hiding place by two women who each took us part of the way. I saw a tall woman with a baby standing next to a fireplace in a house without electric lights. I was expected to be a nanny as well as take care of all the rest of the household chores, along with caring for my brother. We carried buckets of water into this house that had no running water. Every day, I sawed wood for the fireplace, and I once severely lacerated my hand. I was luckier than my brother, because I attended school where I was away from the constant gruff orders and chores. In school I enjoyed the kindness of my teacher, whom I sensed knew that I was a Jew and looked out for me.

But it was another matter for my 3-year-old brother, who had no way to escape and who began to regress from the harsh beatings he received during the day while I was at school. My brother became very fearful, stopped talking, and began to wet his pants. One day I came back from school and saw open wounds on him. The tall woman told me, "Yes, today I taught him. I gave him the pot to pee and shit in, and he did it not in the pot but next to it. I made him eat it." One day she pushed him into the fireplace and I saw his burns right away when I got back from school. Then the woman made him go through the garden to the toilet—a hole in the ground—and he was just a little kid. He could have fallen into it. I knew that my mother paid this family a lot of money for our care; they treated us badly and took the money well. I think this harsh treatment scarred my brother's personality, turning him into a closed and angry person.

Through the minister who had found one of our hiding places, my mother found housing for herself that was closer to us. At first she didn't recognize me because I didn't have any hair, but she recognized me through my eyes. Though I recognized my mother, I met her like a stranger, which was a shocking and immense disappointment to my mother. My brother and I remained at that house until the war was over. I knew that although my mother worried about me, she worried even more about my little brother who was totally dependent on the goodwill of the people we lived with.

I had been out of my house, away from my mother, for 15 months before the war ended. One of the first things we did was to visit my teacher, so that my mother could thank her for showing me such kindness. The three of us moved into a small house with a garden. With advice from neighbors, I grew a vegetable garden from seeds. I remember being so proud of my small garden, especially of the tasty cucumbers.

When I was 20, I immigrated to Israel. I married and had two children, after undergoing treatment for my difficulty conceiving and carrying my pregnancies to term. I believe that my fear of being pregnant stemmed from the sexual abuse I experienced during the Holocaust.

JUDITH

Until the age of six I was one of the happiest children in the world. This is how I saw my life between 1935 and 1941. My father was a very rich man of strong character who owned shops. One was a renowned art shop, and the other, a butcher shop. He supplied his own meat for the butcher shop through a cattle farm he owned and managed outside of town. My mother worked as an administrator in the local Jewish social service organization. We lived on a long street dotted with synagogues and *mikves*, ritual bath houses for Orthodox Jews. Even though my father wasn't very religious, we lived in the Jewish part of town out of respect for, and to accommodate, my maternal grandmother. A widow with five children, she had fled from Galicia, Poland, to escape persecution. My father regarded her as a very smart woman who bravely raised her children on sheer determination. Her only son was killed accidentally by a hunter when he was 18 years old.

In 1940 my mother heard more about how hard things were getting for Jews and that doctors and professors who had money were able to escape to other countries. She tried to convince my father to take our whole family out of the country, but my father didn't want to leave. He thought that he could negotiate with the Germans. My mother's eldest sister married a man from another city, and he advised my father to sell everything and leave. But my father strongly believed that the situation wasn't so dire and things would work themselves out. He even convinced the husband of one of my maternal aunts, who worked with my mother at the service agency, not to flee with his family.

In January 1941, my mother was about to give birth to my baby sister and was afraid for herself and for the baby. She had Christian friends who helped her with the delivery. With their help, she was able to sneak back into her own home with her newborn. When my sister was 4 months old, several days before Passover, soldiers flooded our street. It was my birthday. We had celebrated with lots of family, and it was a happy party. But that night sirens screeched and panic spread. We didn't have shelters so we hid in our basements. It was very crowded; children cried as bombs exploded. The police entered our basement and ordered us to gather in front of the synagogue to receive official directives. These commands involved the subsequent closing of every Jewish business. Jews working in public jobs were immediately fired. Our street became a ghetto, and we had to wear visible yellow tags on our clothing.

By 1942 new orders required that we leave our homes and take only a few personal items intended for a short stay elsewhere. We were transported by truck and transferred into rail cars without windows or air. They pushed us like animals. We were separated—men alone, women alone. I heard a series of gunshots. Later, after arriving at the labor camp, we learned that my father and uncle had dashed out of line in an attempted escape and the guards fired at them. It was assumed they had been killed. My mother and aunt became deeply saddened and withdrawn and remained in that emotional state throughout their four years in the camp.

When we arrived, we were placed in a small cabin with wooden planks for beds and blankets. We worked to clean the cabin because it stank. No one was allowed to wander freely outside. Our whereabouts were under strict control. My mother and aunt were taken to work in a health clinic. Children of six years and older had to work.

I was taken inside a big, repulsively smelling warehouse without windows. On a table there were many teeth of people who died, full of mold and blood. Many children passed out because of this frightful sight, combined with the stench and lack of air. I refused to work because of how badly I felt. The manager reacted to my refusal by slamming my hand with a pole, breaking one of my fingers. I fainted from the pain and was sent to the clinic where my mother worked. The doctor didn't want to operate on my hand, so my mother took a stick and bandaged it.

When I was eight years old, a new manager who was even crueler arrived at the warehouse. If he caught somebody resting or making a mistake, he tortured that child. He selected girls who were 16 or 17 and would take them into a room, sometimes together and sometimes individually. The girls would be gang raped by him and many soldiers. When they came out of that side room into the central room of the warehouse, they were injured and sick. Some came out dead. The girls who survived were often taken care of by my mother in the clinic.

One day I wandered around the camp without telling anyone. I was bored because Jewish children were not allowed to study nor have schooling of any kind. I would try to take scraps of paper and draw. Sometimes I found chips of coal and would use this to draw what I saw around me. On this particular day I wasn't even wearing my patch. At first I went unnoticed because I had blond hair with little curls; the guards assumed I was another guard's daughter.

I grew tired and sat down on a rock, drawing lazily in the dirt with a stick. I saw ants carrying food and pondered why they were free and I wasn't. Then I saw a tall man wearing a black suit and high boots coming up to me along with his dog. The dog was taller than me, and I was scared of the dog, so he told the dog something in German, and the dog sat still. He asked me what I was looking for in the ground. I told him I wasn't looking for anything but had only wanted to walk around. He asked my name and then wanted to know whether or not I was a Jew. When I said that I was, he asked me why I wasn't wearing the patch. I said I'd forgotten. Then he took a big stick and swung in into my face, breaking my nose and several teeth. I was bleeding badly, told him I was sorry, and begged him to let me go. He grabbed me and threw me onto the ground, ordering the dog to attack me. The dog bit me and ripped my clothes off. Then the guard came over to me and burned his cigarette into my face. I screamed so loud, hoping that someone would hear me and help me, but nobody did. Then he put his penis inside my mouth and peed. I started choking and vomiting. So he shot me in my leg, and left me there alone.

I don't remember what happened then or how I survived. I regained consciousness in a strange place with women who were wearing black and white on their heads. I thought that I had died and gone to heaven because I didn't know what nuns looked like. They bandaged me and took care of me. They didn't know that I was Jewish because I was blond. I opened my eyes and started calling mamma, mamma. They asked me who my mother was, so I told them what I knew—I'm at the camp with my family. They got scared because they were not allowed to help Jews. They sent someone to look for my family and brought me back to the camp where my mother and grandmother took care of me. My grandmother knew a lot about healing plants, and from whatever plants she found outside, she made creams to put on my wounds. After this I became a physically scarred girl, with many fears. I stopped eating, I stopped talking, and I didn't want anything anymore.

In 1944, toward the end of the war, that same German guard showed up accompanied by others and ordered my family out of the cabin, exclaiming, "That girl has got to be punished. Her mother lied about her, saying she was her daughter, though she probably stole her from some Christians. So I'll punish her too." My so-called Aryan looks had aroused German suspicions about me and my mother. The guard shouted, "It's your last chance to tell me where you took that girl from." My mom showed him my birth certificate. He took the papers, ripped them up, yelling, "You Jews are all liars! You ruin the world!" Then he forcefully grabbed my little sister, slammed her on a rock, took an ax and chopped her into two pieces. My grandma jumped toward her granddaughter, so he shot her in the head. My mother passed out, and when my aunt went to her aid, he shot her in the head too. I was frozen on the spot, unable to speak.

The next memory that I had was of waking up after the war in a hospital. I could not even recognize my mother who had become an old skinny woman, with white hair and yellowish skin. I cried out that I wanted my mommy, I wanted my grandma, I wanted my sister. After that outburst I went mute again. I remember receiving many injections, pills, and vitamins and being connected to several tubes while the Russians took care of me in a hospital for a full year.

Then, in 1946, my father and uncle, who had joined the Partisans and had been wounded, returned from the war looking for their families. I was eleven. I refused to talk to my father other than to accuse him of being a bad man because he abandoned us, and that's why everything happened, though it wasn't so. After my father heard about what had been done to his family, he became insane and was hospitalized.

I survived but the trauma of extreme persecution left a mark on the rest of my life. After I got out of the hospital, whenever I saw a dog I assumed a fetal position on the floor and wouldn't move until someone came and talked to me and helped me. I couldn't read or write at age 12 because I had never been to school and such learning had been prohibited in the camp. At school, children teased me because of my disfigurements and scars, shouting that I looked like Frankenstein. Afterward, I refused to go to school until a woman counselor came to my house, and my mother told her about what had happened to me. The woman cried even though she wasn't Jewish. This counselor gathered the children in my class together and told them my story. After that nobody harassed me anymore, but I couldn't make any friends. I stayed away from boys because of the image of the soldier's penis in my mouth.

After I arrived in Israel in 1950 I began treatment with a psychologist, and that treatment required a psychiatric hospitalization.

I fell in love with a man but he had an affair with one of my girlfriends. I found out about this after my friend got pregnant and after they had already decided to marry. I was deeply hurt and told myself that I must never trust anyone. But I married someone I didn't love in 1952 when I was 17 so I could leave my parents' house. My father returned from the war a changed man and became an alcoholic. He became physically abusive toward me and my mother. My marriage didn't last past the first night, though. My husband had an epileptic seizure and fell out of bed. When I saw his penis I panicked, ran out of the house, and traveled back to my parents' home. The next day I was hospitalized and afterward I divorced my husband.

I put a wall around myself and didn't socialize. But years later when I was 27, I went to a party, and one man kept trying to talk with me. Eventually, he convinced me to go out with him, and we dated for six months before we got married. I told him that I was married before but had never had sex, and he didn't believe me. On our wedding night I was too frightened to have sex with him. The next day he bought champagne, arranged a table, and encouraged me to drink until I felt easier being touched. When we had sex I bled. He then believed me when I said I had been a virgin, but when I saw the blood I began screaming, "What have you done to me?!" My husband always was sexually gentle and loving, but I was never able to enjoy sex. During the night I would often have nightmares, and my husband would wake me and give me a pill so that I could sleep more restfully. After a year our son was born and not long after, our daughter. A month after our daughter was born I became very depressed and stopped nursing the baby. My husband hired a helper to care for me and to perform household chores. One day I found my husband in bed with this helper. I was shocked because up until then I thought he was the best husband. After my initial shock, I demanded that they both get out of the house. My husband's family appealed to me to forgive him. I allowed him back into the home but not so much into my heart. From then on I did what I wanted.

My husband consulted a psychologist about my paralyzing fear of dogs. The psychologist suggested getting a puppy. For some weeks I couldn't even pet the puppy, but slowly I got used to him. But I remained terrified when I saw large dogs. My husband died of a heart attack at age 45, when I was 51, and I have remained a widow since. During a war in Israel I went into "shock" again, which meant that in 1990 I had to close my hair salon, which I had opened shortly after marrying my second husband.

I've told you what happened to me. I can't say any more.

CORNELIA

The first member of my family to be taken away was my older brother, who was conscripted into the Hungarian army before the Holocaust got underway. I never saw him again. When I was seven in 1944, the Nazis deported me and my family to the ghetto, where we were "housed" in a sugar factory. Everything had been taken from us. My father had been a candy manufacturer, and we had had lived very well in a small quiet Christian town in which Jews were integrated. Our stop in the ghetto was just a waiting point along the conveyor belt to the concentration camps. When the designated train arrived, Nazi guards couldn't forcibly squash another body into it, so my parents and elder siblings—five sisters and two brothers—were transported instead to a concentration camp in Austria. All of my family died in that camp. After the war I immigrated to Israel and married but I never bore children because of the damage done to my body in the camp. I was used as a human guinea pig. The purported "medical experiments" forced on me left me infertile. That's the short version of my story. The longer one is far more difficult for me to tell.

It's tough to describe the Holocaust as no words can explain the suffering from the things they did to us. So I'll begin my story to juxtapose my gentle, protected childhood with what came afterward. I was born in the very hospital that my grandfather had built and contributed to the town. My mother always wanted to live close to her own mother, but after I was born my immediate family moved to a smaller town where about 100 Jewish families lived. I felt very secure because my family was rich, and Jews in general were assimilated, living close to the non-Jews for hundreds of years, thinking that we were the same actually.

The Austrian-Hungarian monarchy had given Jews the right to vote, choose where to live, whatever they wanted—we were equal. Jews were admitted into universities and some became doctors and engineers. Some succeeded in businesses and were among the wealthy in the community. In Jewish homes children didn't know poverty and hunger. My parents' friends as well as my uncle owned factories that employed many people. My other uncle and his wife were doctors. Both my mother and father had graduated from the university. My mother used her cooking skills and know-how to help my father perfect excellent chocolates and manage bookkeeping for our candy factory.

We had a lovely home that still stands and the gentiles even let us visit it on holidays. I remember my father exclaiming, "Why should I go to America? I have everything here." Jews in our community became "modern" and shed their religious traditions. The moderns (like Reform Jews) built the most beautiful synagogues where choirs sang, and we dressed the same as the non-Jews. Jews were accepted or we believed that we were, with four hands, not just two.

My family possessed documents dated 1803 attesting that my mother's great-grandfather was born in that part of Hungary. We held even earlier documents for my father's side of the family. When the Nazis started to deport our family to the ghetto, we thought that our deep roots in the country might enable us to be treated more as citizens, but our documents were summarily ignored.

This perceived acceptance went with the wind in 1938, when restrictions against the Jews started. My father's factory was confiscated and given to Christians to run. In 1939–40 Jews were banned from enrollment in universities. Men were abducted and taken to labor camps. Women, children, and old people remained behind. Some men could send postcards to inform their families that they were still alive. Somehow during this period we lived, in contrast to what happened when the Nazi party, called the Hungarian Cross, entered Hungary.

Hundreds of Jews from my hometown were taken along with my family to the ghetto beside the railway tracks where the sugar factory building stood. My parents were coerced into turning over my mother's beautiful gold box containing jewelry that my father had purchased for her on her birthdays. We had to bring our household valuables to the municipality. On the chilly April morning when we were thrust into the ghetto, I stood alongside my family in front of our house wrapped in my coat. We had packed a parcel according to instructions. I turned to look at the house as we started to walk. My mother held my hand; I looked into my mother's face and started to cry, knowing in my heart that we would never come back. I don't know how a child thinks about stuff like that, but unfortunately we never came back, none of us. We heard that people went into our house and took everything—rugs, piano, furniture, the works.

I will never forget. Hunger began when we entered the ghetto; we had no food. We were taken to the sugar factory and slept right on the floor. My mother worked in the kitchen and secured little things for me to eat. I saw people tortured. Two men who tried to escape were hung in the middle of the factory's square for nearly 24 hours until they died. I thought my mother was beautiful, but I noticed that her hair turned white from the trauma of this time. The morning after the hangings, some Hungarian gendarmes threw several men under a train to be run over.

For weeks the trains came and went, taking away some each time. My mother thought that nothing could be worse, so when the train came for us she wanted the family to get on, even though about 90 people were pushed into one boxcar. There was only one small window with bars and a pot in the middle for people to use as a toilet. The train traveled for days without any distribution of food or water. Sometimes when the train stopped, we shouted for water, but not only did the people outside not give us water, they laughed and shouted, "Finally, they take the Jews." The train took us past Auschwitz. We only stopped there so that the bodies of those who died in transit could be pulled off the train. After all these years I can't forget the smell of the decomposing bodies of children, adults, and elders. I can't explain why we were saved that day (a word that seems to mock what we went through) by the train traveling past Auschwitz and the crematoriums. We were in a state of semi-consciousness from continuously standing with no water or food.

The train stopped in Austria not far from Vienna at a camp that probably held 100,000 people. My family continued to wear the same clothes that we had worn on the train, and we remained parched and hungry. The work day stared at 4 a.m. and this included the children, even the young ones. All the instructions were given in German. One day the SS ordered that the younger children be transported elsewhere. I don't need to tell you how afraid I was. When I saw the soldier come for me, I grabbed my mother's hand to feel safe and protected. My impulse for security in my mother's presence reflected back to my memories of our loving family in our old home. But the guards yanked me away from my mother and took me along with the other young children to a concentration camp. But this camp was so full that we had to go back. This was another time that my life was saved by coincidence, but when I say that, I have no feelings of relief over my own "good luck".

One morning my mother and I were working in the fields when we were surprised to be given some soup and bread. All of a sudden the guards started to yell at us to stand up and to begin marching towards a concentration camp in Austria. We walked many kilometers, several days in a row, with minimal clothing. It was November. Anyone who sat to rest for a while was shot in the head. I can't forget the faces of the people they shot. At first my mother put her hand over my eyes to keep me from seeing these murders. Then she stopped doing that.

Finally we arrived at Mauthausen on a rainy night when we could hardly pick up our feet out of the mud. We saw the SS guards and heard their repeated commands to hurry up through the gates of the camp. They threw clothes with stripes at us and gave me adult-size sandals that my legs were too tired to lift. I slept on the mud in tents with some of my siblings and my mother, who hugged us to her.

For several months at this camp we went through hell—indescribable suffering, threats, and hunger. Every day we had to stand up for hours. Those who fell down were strangled. They did medical experiments on us, especially on children. They undressed me, spread my legs, and gave me some shots in my vagina. I fainted, I think. Afterward, they might have thought I was dead and threw me in a wagon to burn my body. During the night I woke to find corpses being thrown on top of me. Jews were compelled to help the Germans with this gruesome work by collecting the corpses after the Nazis killed them. I cried out, "Mommy, Mommy" and suddenly felt that I had some air to breathe. A man lifted me and put me into the children's shack. That means I stayed alive. To this day I don't know who saved me. I think my mother looked for me day and night but could not find me because she was prohibited from walking between sub-camps. In the children's shack, typhus, fleas and diarrhea spread amongst us. And always there were the experiments. Every time they spread my legs apart and put something into my vagina it was so painful. I didn't even have the strength to cry any more. I don't even know all of what they did to me because I would faint from the pain. It burned me and for hours I couldn't stand up. I was full of blood and bleeding most of the time. My belly hurt so much, I couldn't eat or drink. I hardly remember eating for months. My legs were so thin they looked like matchsticks to me. The bottoms of my feet where so swollen that I couldn't even put them into big shoes, and I had no strength to lift the shoes. At the age of seven and eight, I saw myself as growing old. At night I had a dream that I was looking for my mother and in the morning my pillow was wet with tears. When I woke up, I wondered why my pillow was wet. I knew that I had to forget about my mother.

Other experiments involved using children to arouse each other sexually. We were just small kids and had no living signs any more. They forced one 14-year-old (there were others) to penetrate me. I didn't respond but just cried like a kitten mewing. I just wanted to drink, I was so thirsty, and hungry all the time. A child younger than me cried too when he was raped by another child who was forced to do so by the guards.

All this had happened in just one year. It was in May 1945 when someone held my hand and asked me to go up to someone else and request food. My senses were turned off; while I could take in the reality of this coaxing, I didn't feel anything just as when it rained or snowed I didn't feel wet or cold. I wasn't in this world anymore. When someone asked where I was going, I would reply automatically that I was going to ask for food. My body at eight and a half was just bones and skin, covered with inflammations, sores, and flea bites. I moved like a robot because others thought I was going to be shot for asking. They gave me some bread. I think it was because they knew that the Americans were near.

On May 4, 1945, Americans arrived at the camp. One of them entered the children's shack, declaring that we were free to leave and that there was no more electric current in the fences. Even after he said, "Go, you are free!" believe me, no one stood up. I don't remember how many times that soldier said again and again, "You can go out" before we, children overcame our fear and eventually walked through the doors. The truth is I didn't care. Think of the fears of what a child is going through over a year in these places. I can't tell you everything. I can't tell the world that I never ever had a doll in my hands again.

Outside, I saw different uniforms than those of the SS. Even then, a couple of the SS grabbed a few guns and shot some Jews. I saw the Americans open up the warehouses, and we attacked the food. We started to eat everything, and some choked and died. I was given a piece of bread but couldn't swallow it and almost choked myself. The American liberators saw how bug infested we were and brought in gas canisters to spray DDT over our nude bodies. It was humiliating, but we were released.

They took us children for medical care in Austria. I had trouble standing and I had a million wounds. Though doctors started to treat them, my health as well as that of the other children remained precarious even when the doctors discharged us from the hospital. Railways had been destroyed at the end of the war, so we were transported in wagons to Hungary. The Joint Distribution Committee met us there and took us to Budapest.

I didn't find any of my family alive. After searching and searching for my parents and other people in my family, I found no one. No uncles or aunts, no cousins, no one. Why didn't I deserve to have at least one person left from the beautiful family that I had?

With the Joint Distribution Committee's help, I was brought to Israel. It took me two years to recover somehow. I was afraid of any noise, I startled easily, I did not speak and I never smiled. I felt ill all the time; I had no hair; and my metabolism had slowed to such a point that I stopped developing physically. Slowly, after two years, my health started to improve and I started to speak again. I ate better and started to grow a little. I should have been in first grade in 1944 but didn't begin school until I was 10.

I graduated though from grade school and even high school. I was a good student because I did everything that was expected, but I always felt like an outsider, as if I wasn't alive. When friends laughed, I never laughed. During those first years in Israel, others would ask me how I got here and I would try to tell them a bit about the concentration camps, but it seemed that no one could understand it. I couldn't talk about my memories or explain that I did not feel alive. Most of the time I kept silent and never spoke about any of my family members who disappeared. After graduating from high school, I started a job and got married. But because of the sexual abuse and torture during the war, I couldn't have children. Doctors couldn't make me fertile so that I could give birth to a child who would be a free person in the world.

I wonder how I unconsciously absorbed what happened to me as such a young child. The minute they put the Jewish star on me I was no longer a Hungarian citizen. They had denied me life. There was no one to protect me. Everyone could do with me what they wanted to—kill me, shoot me, and commit any fantasy of torture. Anyone could do anything to me.

They didn't have to ask anyone, because to a Jew or to a Jewish child they were allowed to do everything and anything. Anything I say about this is grossly inadequate and cannot even start to express what we went through. You cannot believe what happened in the Holocaust, in how many ways people can kill people. I witnessed terrible things—vaginas taken out of women without anesthetics, people bleeding to death. I remember seeing a child who was injected with air and who screamed in agony. I hear these screams at night and I am not sure whether I am the one screaming or whether I am hearing the agony of others. I wake up with these shouts still ringing in my ears and I find myself trembling all over. These traumas are with me all the time. I have the same thoughts, the same memories. I wonder whether God helped me or didn't help me by keeping me physically alive. I don't know whether to say thank you or not.

But I have a role to play because we are the last of the Survivors. I have friends who as Survivors are not willing to tell their own stories. My husband died and I live alone. I'm not healthy and I fell down a little while ago after fainting in the street. But we must speak. We must make sure that the State of Israel will always exist. To make sure this will never happen again and that no one can ever be killed just because he or she is a Jew.

DUNIA

I've put on earrings for my interview but this doesn't make me feel special. When people tell me that I am an attractive woman, I shrink inside myself to nothing. I can't accept compliments about my art that I make from scraps of old rags, and I can't accept gratitude for the advice I give someone. I'm always left feeling smaller than an ant. Maybe it was because they plundered my life and my body and tore me open. Even after I had had 12 operations to repair my cervix, the doctors told my adoptive kibbutz mother that I would not be able to bear children. I walked around with the feeling that I would never be a mother, and asked myself, what am I worth and why did they do this to me?

I was born into a family rich in Jewish tradition and learning. My father studied the Bible and Rashi's commentary on the Talmud. He spoke and wrote precise Hebrew and Yiddish. My mother, who had completed high school, which was unusual for a girl in their town, taught us to read at a young age. We often read to ourselves and aloud to each other. My father and mother married through a *shidech*, or arranged marriage. My father and grandfather peddled clothing and fabrics in nearby villages from a horse-drawn wagon. My father gave defective material to me because my "good hands" could fix all kinds of flaws and tears in the cloth. I learned this from my grandmother, who made dolls for her granddaughters using scrap materials. We named the dolls according to Yiddish storybook characters and used them to act out our imagined stories. In one of our stories, my doll had a niece in the United States who sent us packages of beautiful clothes including high-heeled shoes.

I was born in 1933. When I was nine years old in 1942, my family and Jewish neighbors were expelled permanently from their homes. We didn't know this at the time because the Romanian soldiers who wanted to loot our houses warned us that our town was going to be bombed and that we should leave our homes for a few hours to hide in the field and return after the bombardment. The soldiers told us not to bother taking any belongings with us. Luckily, my mother sensed that we would not be returning home so quickly. She gathered together all our jewelry and money and hid it in between the clothes we carried. By doing this, she saved us from starving for some time until the money ran out. I was studying music at the time, and I walked out of our house with my precious mandolin pressed against me.

For a while our extended family was in a ghetto where we were given little food. Many people became sick with typhus, lice, and scabies. They forced my father and grandfather into a compulsory labor camp, but my grandfather escaped and rejoined us. Before and after the ghetto, my family repeatedly fled from town to town searching for food and trying to avoid capture, eventually crossing the border from Romania into the Ukraine. With each escape things got worse. Wherever we went we traded our money and jewelry for food. I even exchanged my mandolin for a loaf of bread. In a small town I contracted typhus for the first time. They had no medicines to treat my high fever, vomiting, diarrhea and convulsions.

When we fled to the next town we faced truly life-threatening danger, hunger, and exposure. There were fourteen of us, including my two sisters, mother, grandfather, aunt, and cousins. We had no more money or jewelry to barter, and we were surrounded by danger and threatened at every turn. Ukrainian soldiers might discover and shoot us; gangs of anti-Semites hunting for fleeing and hiding Jews could attack us; local farmers, from whom we would look for food or a day's work, could harm or kill us by raping, stoning, charging their dogs, or turning us over to the Nazis. Our goal was survival—finding a potato here or there, begging farmers for a slice of bread, performing the most menial labor in exchange for something to eat.

Our clothes were in shreds, and we had no place to live. When we walked through the farmers' lands, they wore swastikas. Our family constantly scavenged for pieces of torn clothing, sacks, and newspapers to sew together to cover ourselves and protect our feet from the snow. We took clothes off Jewish corpses. These people had died from murder, hunger, or disease. Local people would openly have sex with female corpses. Our family made needles from twigs and mended and pieced together shreds of clothing we found. We slept in woods, fields, and barns. For the most part, we lived out in the open, and when someone found a plank, that became the "bed" for the person who was the sickest at the time. We tried to pick our teeth clean of food particles, because otherwise while we slept rats were attracted to them and would bite our mouths. Everyone became covered with lice, both black and white varieties, as well as genital lice, bedbugs, and engorged ticks. We cut each other's hair with scissors that my mother miraculously found, but no matter how short we cut our hair, lice and ticks still found us. My skin was covered by inflammations from malnutrition. My family had several types of typhus, and I had a couple of types as well as hepatitis.

At first we had strength to walk and fan out each morning to look for any menial work that could help us bring back a slice of bread. Before we parted to go our separate ways each day, we would kiss and hug each other, because we never knew who would come back. But as time passed we lost even the strength to be affectionate. My mother proclaimed to the family, "We know that we are all of one heart, so from now on we won't hug and kiss each other and we don't need to talk. We will save our last strength to get somewhere to work during the day for a piece of bread."

I worked for one farmer who looked for Jewish children for work because she knew that they worked hard. I tended the chickens. This farmer threw garbage at me, but I still think she saved me from time to time because the pig manure that she threw often landed on my face and disguised my Jewish origins. My grandfather and I often looked for work together; once we came upon a lady without teeth holding a loaf of bread in her armpit. We looked at it and both of us started drooling. This lonely lady use to cut very thin slices of bread for my grandfather and me as we listened to her troubles and worked on her farm. She told us that her husband and four sons had been slaughtered during World War I.

Once, as I moved from farm to farm looking for work, the smell of fresh bread came to my nose and it was like I was drunk. I can smell that smell right now. I was attracted to it like a magnet. I started to walk toward that smell, and entered the house that the smell came out from. The house was warm and the stove was on. I must have fainted, because my next memory is of being on the floor with my head facing the ceiling and all the members of the household looking down at me as if I were an alien. I figured that they knew I was a Jew and I was afraid they would kill me. But instead they asked me to have a seat. I saw pieces of cloth from military blankets stacked in a corner of the room. The head of the household turned out to be a tailor who sewed coats from these scraps. I took a couple of small pieces, sewed them together quickly to form a doll to hand to the beautiful little girl with a round face like the moon and red cheeks from the warmth of that house. They gave me a piece of the fresh, warm bread, but I was scared and didn't know what to do with it. I knew that 14 members of my family were waiting in the woods and that I should give them the piece of bread rather than eat it all by myself. So I ate one bite after another and told them I needed work.

Out of pity they took me to the yard and told me to dig animal feed out of the frozen ground. I did this with my hands after first removing the snow from the ground. I saw that some of the feed had been partially eaten by animals and I thought that if it was good for them it should be good for me. I took bites and then covered the bitten portion with mud so that it would look as if an animal had disturbed the feed. After several days the people at the farm told me that they couldn't continue to allow me to be on their property because it was too dangerous for them to have any connection with a Jew.

I remember that one farmer I worked for gave his dog a pot of leftovers at the end of the day. I drooled when I saw all that milk, pork, and bread mixed together. I remember drooling and wishing I could be a dog. One day, as I tried to get close to the dog and his food, he bit me. Though I was raised to observe Jewish dietary laws prohibiting eating milk with meat, I was ready to eat anything.

As my family roamed the countryside, we stepped on corpses and saw dogs eating parts of dead Jews. One day I saw a dog with a skull in his mouth that still had a scarf wrapped around it. The patterned scarf was like the one my friend's mother wore. I saw a friend cutting her wrists vigorously with an iron she had found. My friend died right in front of us.

My mother believed in God and told us children that it was because of God that our family remained alive. My grandfather with his deep faith in God motivated me and other family members to hold onto hope. My grandfather didn't let me give up. He was our rescuing angel and kept some of our family alive through his pure faith, humility, and simplicity and his recitation of inspiring Psalms. To this day, I believe that he was one of the secret righteous men of the world. (A Jewish mystical belief conceives that there are 36 hidden righteous people in each generation that assure the continuity of the world).

My sturdy grandfather never got sick and worked wherever he could, even in pigpens, for a bit of food for his family. The stench from pig dung is so vile that you can never forget it, a stench that sticks to every pore of your body and it remained with me my entire life. But my grandfather did not flinch even though he was a deeply religious man. The Jewish religion forbids eating pig meat, but he still took care of the pigs. He prayed three times a day, every day, no matter what. I worked alongside my grandfather in the pigpens during a winter with deep snows. The two of us brought back bits of food to our family's hideaways every day to feed my mother and sisters—a few frozen carrots or beets, crumbs of bread—and even on these meager leftovers my grandfather bestowed the traditional Jewish blessings of gratitude. I remember that he had a shaven head with a round dark purple circle on his scalp from a piece of metal that had lodged in his skull during World War I. Before the Holocaust, my grandfather used to tell his grandchildren war stories and we lovingly stroked that purple spot on his head.

One time my grandfather returned to the family with a rusty can filled with whey. The whey could have revived our starving bodies a bit. Defiantly, my grandmother got up from her sickbed plank, turned over the can, and spilled the whey in the snow, announcing that it was Passover and that the whey was *chametz* (leavened food that is prohibited on Passover). I was enraged! I wanted to strangle her for her selfish act.

One Sunday in 1943 my grandfather and I worked for the same farmer. While my grandfather cleaned out the pigpen, I sat in a wood shack not far from him mending holes made by rats in corn sacks. The church bells rang and the farmer's family, dressed in fancy black clothes, promenaded off to church. I regarded them as looking so noble, all of them with their blond hair and blue eyes. In particular, I watched the pretty mother and wife named Olga strolling in a long black dress with a black silk scarf over her shoulders. I compared this image to my mother's, so emaciated yet swollen by hunger, and I wondered why my mother couldn't dress like that and besides had to starve.

Even after the farmer's family left, my grandfather and I were afraid to talk to each other in Yiddish in case someone would overhear us and know that we were Jews. After almost another hour of sewing the sacks, I heard steps in the snow. The steps got closer and closer, and then they stopped right near me. I saw shiny black boots and I was too afraid to look up. My grandfather had already been whacked in the head by a bar and lay unconscious in the snow, but I didn't know that until later. Apparently, it was the farmer who had left his family on the way to church and backtracked with his son. He grabbed my gaunt 10-year-old body while I still held the sack that I was darning, raised me up into the air and flung me with all his might onto the floor among the sacks. I still remember the smell from his mouth. As he violently raped me, he clamped my mouth shut. After he was through, he turned me over to his son. The son bit into my inner thigh near my genitals ripping off a chunk of my flesh, leaving a scar that will remain with me until the day I die. They left quickly. I don't know whether they rejoined their family in church.

I was left lying with the sack rolled up around my neck and blood on my thighs. I had no feeling, or at least no words to explain how I felt. I didn't understand what had happened to me. I thought I might have been killed and that this is how a person dies; soon I expected not to see or hear. When that didn't happen, I tried to get up but couldn't. I tried to yell "Papa," the name I used for my grandfather, and crawled for some distance toward the pigpen, unable to stand up. My lower body hurt, but though I had heard about rape before, I was so young that I didn't understand that what had happened to me was rape. I put some snow in my mouth to wet my throat. My blood combined with the man's ejaculation didn't drip but congealed instantly because it was so cold out. I desperately and repeatedly rubbed the snow on my skin to clean myself with my last bit of strength.

But Papa did not answer. Finally I saw him lying in the pigs' mire with his face covered with congealed blood. His lips were blue, his glasses were smashed, and he was dead, no doubt. But I couldn't accept it so I started frantically pummeling him in the chest with my little fists. I pinched him and bit him, yelling, "Get up, wake up! Wake up! Get up! Don't leave me alone. We can't die! Everyone is waiting for us, waiting for the bread!" I didn't know how to wake up my Papa, but I remembered stories about his World War I wound. I was feeling desperate to do something, so I bit the blue patch of skin over the metal piece in his skull with all my might. The piece of metal from 1915 fell out, and my grandfather opened his eyes. He didn't know where he was or what happened, but somehow we dragged ourselves through the snow until we reached the rest of our family. My grandfather told them, "The deed has been done to her." That was what they said in Yiddish when women and girls of all ages were raped.

My experiences led me to think all Jewish females were raped. After my own rape, the rest of my family and I witnessed my maternal aunt being gang raped by a group of Ukrainian youths who preyed on escaping Jews. When they were not participating in the rape, they stood guard with cubs and bats, ready to kill any family members who tried to help her. My aunt screamed all kinds of incomprehensible words before losing consciousness. The rape left her psychotic, and her lower body was paralyzed. She would drag herself on the ground and became an easy target for flocks of rats that bit her.

Not long after this, my aunt's little daughter died from typhus. My grandfather tore part of his lice-covered coat in order to wrap the toddler's body, to treat her remains with dignity. We tried to rub off some of the lice with snow, but it did no good. We dug into the snow-covered ground with our hands to try to bury our little cousin deep enough so she wouldn't be eaten by roving dogs. This child, Mina, was 1½ at the time we were expelled from our homes. My aunt nearly died giving birth to her. This was her only precious child following the death of her firstborn. After she was raped, my aunt did not even ask where her daughter was or show any signs that she knew of Mina's death or disappearance.

Next, it was my mother who was raped. She never told us about it, but the signs were all there. She had searched as usual for menial day labor one morning and returned that same day a very different person. She had had gold teeth and returned that night toothless, with black and blue marks across her face and body. She was silent and rarely spoke after that day. The rape left her pregnant, but she didn't realize it throughout most of her pregnancy. The women ate so little that they stopped menstruating, so she did not know that she had conceived. And because we were all scrawny and shriveled, she, like the rest of the women, did not have signs of a stomach or enlarged breasts that would have signaled to her that she was pregnant. But after liberation, when our family returned to our hometown, my mother started to feel movement inside of her and knew she'd be delivering. My half-brother was born on April 17, 1945.

My mother did not have the physical or emotional stamina to raise this baby. I didn't know whether she loved her son or not, but I think that he reminded my mother of her disgrace and trauma. The baby was born prematurely. My mother started to bleed and hemorrhage so much that she almost died. She was saved by having a hysterectomy in a hospital in Brasov, Romania where she recuperated for 6 months. Meanwhile, the baby boy was cared for by my older sister. We hardly had any food to give him, so we used to soak pieces of bread with a little sugar, and that was what he sucked.

My father returned from the forced-work camp. Unlike my kindly mother and grandfather, I saw my father as a self-centered man who did not love his daughters or his wife, yet he was crazy over his son and pampered him, setting no limits. After my mother's rape my parents did not live together as husband and wife. I think my mother felt that she was defiled. Many years later my father started to dress well and had other women while my mother wore shabby, tattered dresses. My father had been saddened at the birth of each of his three daughters because he wanted a son to pass on his name. He adopted this son as his own and named him Aaron after his father. Aaron was unruly and probably hyperactive, making raising him a challenge. To make matters worse, after the Holocaust my parents' spiritual strength was depleted and they had practically nothing to feed him, either.

I came alone on Aliyah to Israel with the illegal immigration in 1947, four years earlier than my parents. I lived in a kibbutz with an organized group of orphans, most of whose parents had been killed in the Holocaust. Unlike the other young girls, I was exempt from serving in the army because during my periods I hemorrhaged severely and had to be given blood transfusions. Even dancing could trigger my bleeding, and this was before the days of sanitary napkins. I remember one day when the blood reached my shoes. I was hospitalized and given six units of blood that the other teenagers in our youth group donated to me. This was the first of 12 operations needed to stitch up my torn cervix.

Because of my internal wounds, I worked sitting down, in the laundry room, ironing for half the day after attending school for the other half. I was a good student in the kibbutz school and quickly began to read Hebrew. It was important to me to learn the language fluently. I sang at parties and events and was given voice-training lessons. Each time I sang I trembled in embarrassment. I needed sedatives to get me through performances.

I was 18 and loved the kibbutz, but my dream of remaining a member withered after my parents, along with my younger sister Miriam and David, made Aliyah in 1952. These four lost souls fell upon me at the kibbutz. My parents had heart disease and swollen legs. I rushed about helping them to get settled, including setting up a kosher kitchen for them. My hyperactive brother threw a ball in the dining room and broke the stacked plates. After just two months, the kibbutz representatives informed me that my family could not remain on the kibbutz. They offered to give them transport and move their things to a transit camp for new immigrants.

At the transit camp, I helped my parents set up their tent, and I visited them every month to bring them whatever food and clothing I could. Eventually, I felt compelled to leave the kibbutz and join my parents in the transit camp where I worked as an assistant to the kindergarten teacher. Whatever few pennies my sister and I earned, we turned over to my father. My father had broken his legs while planting and pruning trees, so he could not work any more. He had also lost a lot of blood through his hemorrhoids and was diagnosed as anemic. His remedy for anemia was to drink a lot of red wine, while the rest of the family, excluding his son, hardly had a piece of bread to eat. I saw my silent and depressed mother along with my sister and myself as servants for my dictatorial father and out-of-control and favored brother.

It wasn't long before my parents started to pester me about getting married to a 37-year-old man who lived with his mother and sister as our neighbors in the transit camp. He had fled Iraq with them after his sister was raped and severely beaten during the anti-Jewish riots in Baghdad. He worked as a clerk in the health clinic in the transit camp. I told my mother about the operations I'd had and that I was probably not able to have children, but still my parents wanted to see me married.

This educated, bald-headed man who knew several languages began to court me, wooing me with promises to treat me like a queen and teach me English and math. He persisted in telling me he was the one for me. In response to this pressure to marry a man I didn't love, I decided to kill myself by swallowing poisonous seeds of the castor tree until I passed out. I was found and was taken to the hospital, where I stayed for two weeks after my stomach was pumped. Not knowing which was worse, to be under the rule of my dictatorial father or to be married to a man who was nearly my father's age, I finally gave into to the latter.

But during the mikva, or ritual bath, required before consummating the marriage, I flung the symbolic marriage ring into the mikva. On my wedding night, the man who promised to treat me like a queen vowed to return me to my parents if I was not a virgin. I went like a lamb to the slaughter. My husband frequently raped me vaginally and anally, abusing me like a psychopath. He made it a point to let me often know that he betrayed me with high-society prostitutes.

After two or three months my periods stopped. I was pregnant! But the freedom not to worry about when and how much I would bleed and not to carry cotton rags with me wherever I went, gave me a feeling of being reborn. I had other worries, though. I had to stand in line to get my food allotment, which I always gave to my mother-in-law, who cooked on a paraffin stove for herself and her two children, giving only the leftovers to me. I weighed 48 kilos [about 106 pounds] and was afraid I was starving my fetus so that it would die before it was born or become a monster like my brother.

To add to these worries, once while I was waiting in the food line on behalf of my in-laws, my sister in-law pushed me down into a rock, and my stomach turned black and blue. When I delivered, the medical staff couldn't believe that a baby of 3½ kilos [7 pounds, 11 ounces] came out of my emaciated body.

My husband, the new father, did not come to the hospital to visit me and our newborn son or take us home from the hospital. I thought my husband acted true to his words that he needed a wife to be his servant and his whore. He continued to rape me every day and night, he totally ignored our son, and he had a mistress whom he also got pregnant.

When my son was a year old, I left and returned to live with my parents under my father's thumb. My mother made chicken soup exclusively for her husband. She would sneak some of his soup to bring to my little son. I said that if my father had discovered this, he would have strangled my mother and me. Once, my own husband caught my mother bringing a small pot of soup and a chicken leg for my son. He grabbed the soup from her and spilled it onto the ground, shouting, "Why do you bring food to my wife? I support her honorably." The truth was that though he had a good job translating Arabic into Hebrew, my son and I lived in a tin hut. Secretively, I cleaned houses far away from the transit camp so that he wouldn't find out, in order to earn money to support myself and my child.

My husband came around often enough to rape me. Sometimes he visited with his mistress, expecting me to serve them what little food I had. I prayed to get pregnant again to have another son, not a daughter who could be raped. This prayer was answered, three years after the birth of my first son. But when my husband found out I was pregnant, he reacted by beating my son and me. I needed blood transfusions because I bled during my second pregnancy. Even though I was weak, I needed to support myself and my son. I began to work as an assistant to the nursery teacher and loved interacting with the children. The teachers and their aides invited me to lunch and insisted that I eat, so now I had food every day and my second son, Uri, was born with a weight of 4½ kilos [9 pounds, 14 ounces].

My husband continued to rape and smack me around and to punish our sons with his fists. He vowed that he would never give me a divorce or allow me custody of his children. When I turned to my father for shelter with the understanding that I'd pay rent, my father told me that since I was a married woman, he had no responsibility toward me. I put a knife under my pillow, and as my husband came to rape me again, I held the knife and vowed that I didn't care if I had to live in solitary confinement the rest of my life—he would never touch me again. I believe I scared him, and I was finally able to divorce him after 11 years of marriage. I gave up all rights to any of our possessions, but I held on to our two sons.

. . .

After talking about the Holocaust and what it did to me, I couldn't sleep for a week. I never sleep well, but by talking about these things, my slightly scabbed wound reopened and I felt engulfed by painful feelings. All my adult life I have been prescribed sedatives. I tried many times to wean myself off the need for those pills. I tried homeopathy, special diets, herbs, yet every time my whole body shakes, and then I give in.

Not even an addiction to sedatives could keep my younger sister alive. My sister had married a wonderful man, and they managed to travel abroad every year at a time when most people couldn't afford it. She refused to take reparations money. Nor did my sister allow anyone to talk about the Holocaust in her presence. My sister tried to kill herself several times, and in 1999 she finally succeeded. I miss her terribly. I try to comfort myself by sifting through her many writings, including songs my sister had composed. Today, one of my sister's sons is CEO of a world-famous transportation company. I wish that my sister could be with me to see what he has accomplished.

TOVA

I have published my autobiography but I did not reveal the sexual abuse I had endured during the Holocaust. I was afraid that my children would read it, and I did not want them to know. The men who raped me were also the ones who helped keep me alive. The first man who did so managed to keep me in the ghetto while my whole family was sent to a concentration camp. Maybe it wasn't so bad because that family that I was sexually abused by—actually saved my life.

In 1939, when I was 10 years old, my parents, my two younger brothers and I were deported from our home in Poland to the Lodz ghetto. We worked each day and lived with a married couple and their three-year-old daughter in the same living quarters. My parents got sick, so the Nazis scheduled them and my brothers for transport to Auschwitz in 1942. I wanted to go with my family but my parents urged me to stay behind. The young mother we lived with assured me not to worry and not to be afraid to stay with them until my parents returned. The young mother was a pharmacologist, and somehow because of her profession, the couple had worked out a special relationship with the Germans. They received more oil for heat and more food and were under less surveillance. Hardly any children were left in the ghetto. Every time there was a selection, they opened a closet and hid their child in it. Other parents were told that their children were to be taken to work. The parents didn't want to let their children go, but the Nazis forcibly grabbed the children from their parents' arms, clubbing the parents as they did so. I remember how parents cried after their children.

While the pharmacologist wife was out of the house out, her husband raped me. I was 13. He was a handsome young man, and he and his wife were very cultured and intelligent people. I remember crying and knowing that if my parents had been there it wouldn't have happened. But the truth is that for a bit of warmth and bread, I think I would have done it anyway. How should I relate to that as rape, since he had actually saved me? I could have gone with my parents and died, but this was also a kind of death.

I would listen to the couple talking during the two years that I remained with them, and they would repeatedly agree that as long as they could keep their daughter, life would be worth living. If their little girl was ever in danger, they intended to commit suicide with the medicine they kept aside. Long afterwards, I met a person in Tel Aviv who had seen the family being sent to the camp. She told me she saw both of them holding their child and slipping something into the toddler's mouth as well as their own when the Germans were about to take the child. They died on the spot. They kept their child to the end. As for me, I don't have any family.

About eight months before I was taken to a concentration camp, I was compelled to work in a clothes factory, mostly with other children. As I walked toward the factory, my friend, who was 10 years older, held my hand as if she were my mother. A Jewish man, whom the Germans made one of the foremen, came up to us, introducing himself as an engineer. He told me that I looked like his wife and he could arrange for the two of us to have better jobs. I immediately understood what he was after, given the past relationship with that man who saved me. But my friend immediately exclaimed, "Good! Great!" The engineer went about asking others the insinuating question, "Look, doesn't she resemble my wife?" I was broken, totally broken.

I told the Jewish foreman to leave me be. But my friend was standing beside me and exclaimed that we had accepted his offer to arrange a better job. When I protested again, the man said, "This is war. I'll give you an easier job and some food." Then he came around, told me and my friend to wash ourselves and then he used us for his sexual needs. I didn't want to have sex, but it seemed that we had no other choice. What do you think he did, a Jew? He did the same like the Germans. I got better food from a German guy.

When we first arrived at this factory, Germans soldiers ordered the girls and women to undress in front of them before they commanded them into the shower. A German woman dressed in white used a 500-watt light bulb to examine our bodies and to shave off all of our hair everywhere. I was so skinny that I didn't have much hair. My friend who was 10 years older than me had nice breasts, though. Two or three German men loudly and lustfully judged my friend's naked body, to her great embarrassment. I tried to hide my friend behind me. I saw how they laughed with such joy to see the girls naked. Some of them raped some of the girls, right in front of everyone else.

I already knew about Auschwitz and Treblinka but was hoping that my parents had been sent to work in a factory, as well. When I asked about them, the German and Jewish foremen laughed at me, saying I was dumb, exclaiming that they were all dead.

One day, a German soldier who was also an engineer approached and ordered us to pick up our clothes and walk through the fields to another factory, a long way away. The soldiers who herded us openly killed some of us as we walked along. Who would say anything? No one cared. This engineer soldier didn't look into my eyes when he raped me. Although he was a very brutal man, somehow I imagine that I was able to keep his viciousness at bay by being a good worker, making bullets and doing everything he asked me to do sexually. I saw his wife and daughters. They were very beautiful. I told him that my cousin (really my friend) knew how to sew. Nearly every night after working in the factory, my friend was taken to sew clothes for his wife. Everyone feared this man including my friend and me, but in the end he was the one who saved us.

One day, all the forced laborers were ordered out of the factory and told to begin walking. This was the death march. But this German soldier had my friend, me, and another girl stay behind in the shack until we could be found by the Americans. I remember how hard it was for me to believe that the cruelest person we knew remembered what my friend (who had sewed for his wife) and I had done for him and saved us both. There were others who had used us for sex, including the Jewish foreman, who had not provided for us. It doesn't matter if men are German or Jews, all men are rapists. All of them knew that these children and young women were going to die, so when they had a chance, that's their nature . . . to take advantage.

The rapes took place in the face of the loss of my family, our abiding hunger, and the wide-ranging tortures we and others endured. I was in such a shock that I didn't care much where I was, what people said to me, and whether I was raped or not. I was finished.

I never spoke about being raped during the Holocaust. We inmates spent our time thinking about food because we were starving. I think the Germans did what they did to us because when a person is hungry, you can do whatever you want with him. When you are hungry, have no bread, whether you die or are raped, it is all the same. Death is not just being shot at. Being raped is death. I remember looking up into the sky above the labor camp and asking God, what happened here? I never saw a cat, a dog, or a bird. I thought maybe they all died because they didn't have anything to eat. The world is dead, I thought, and no one cares.

After the war I was all alone. I still expected someone from my family to return, because I had come from such a large extended family. But there was no one. Later, I discovered one of my uncles who had survived, married a non-Jew, and lived in Chile. They never had much contact with me. I knew that many children were alone and orphaned. With the help of the Jewish agency, I was brought in a roundabout way to Israel. First I went to Naples, Italy, and boarded a ship headed for Alexandria, Egypt. From there we navigated through the British blockade and docked in Haifa.

I left Europe without any pictures, any evidence of my family before the war. It wasn't easy for me to make the transition in 1947, but at least we had bread. The need to work from morning to night might have forced me to get healthy. I worked all the time, too, so I would be too busy to think. I had nothing, came with nothing. Working hard from morning to night saved me.

Now, when I'm not always so busy I can't stop the invading memories and sometimes I think I'm losing my mind. Those thoughts have led me many times to consider killing myself. Sometimes when I think about my life, I tell myself that nothing happened. Other times I ask myself again and again how I could have been born into a safe, loving family and then gone through hell. Every year, before the beginning of our living nightmare, my family used to vacation in the forest for two months during summer. We rented a house. My mother was happy. We all ate and had cows and horses; it was great.

I don't know why my well-off family waited until the Germans invaded rather than escape to Russia. Two non-Jews had come to my father to advise him that he could still leave with his wife and children. He graciously thanked the two men for their kindness in thinking about us under such circumstances. But he declined, explaining, "Maybe you will not understand, but I worked hard all these years in our factory, and it's mine. How will I take my children through the field without food?" This killed us. Even as a young girl at the time, I thought my father should have agreed, because I already saw Germans shooting through windows. I remembered that my parents used to say that Germans were a cultured and intelligent people who would never do things like that. It didn't take long before they shut our family into the ghetto and my father saw his mistake. My father took it hard that he made this mistake. He wanted to die. He stayed in bed and didn't want to work until they were taken to die in Auschwitz.

Years after coming to Israel, I married but I never wanted to get pregnant. I tried to abort my pregnancy. My doctor told me I shouldn't because of the small number of Jews that remained alive.

I don't believe in any man. If they have an opportunity, they will throw you down. A woman who will give herself away is one who has already been hurt badly. Maybe rape isn't so bad; maybe I should be glad. After all, my rapists, including the young refined handsome man in the ghetto, the Jewish foreman, and the sadistic German engineer soldier, were also my saviors. My thoughts about these rapes churn in me: were they rapists or saviors? Am I truly alive? And is that a good thing or not? Other plaguing questions run rapid fire through my mind. Who would think that such a thing like the Holocaust could happen? What are people thinking when they are cremated alive? What did my parents think? We have a country for the Jews, but how many Jews are not here?

AFTERWORD

Hearing the horrific stories of these seven Survivors was acutely painful for us. Yet, we realized that only now, as social work professionals of middle age, were we able to really listen to them. Born of the generation in the wake of the Holocaust, we identify with the Survivors' pain and suffering. We also feel extremely lucky to have been born after the war, one of us in Israel and the other in the United States, where we hope nothing like the Holocaust will ever happen again.

But there is no doubt that the trauma of the Holocaust was passed down to us. The fear that this horror might happen again, the need to fight anti-Semitism, the need to stay close to other Jews, the need to remember the Holocaust and make sure that it is never forgotten, and to tell our children, the third generation, about it—all of this has been indelibly part of who we are. The Holocaust was a monumental upheaval, the effect of which reverberates through the lives of Survivors, their families, and their communities. We feel therefore compelled to share some of our reactions and experiences in developing this book with you, the reader, and have chosen to do this in the form of a dialog:

Rachel: Both my mother and father were Child Survivors of the Holocaust and this became a significant part of my identity. I saw myself in the way that Vardi described the second generation of Holocaust Survivors: a memorial candle for the Holocaust.

Susan: My parents and most of my extended family were not in the Holocaust. The Holocaust loomed large in my mind as a child, but because I was not a child of Survivors, there were no labels for me. I had no descriptive composite to validate my associations, fears, and commitments. Only recently, have we begun to understand that such a horror is collectively experienced in some aspects and is transmitted down through the generations.

Rachel: Even though I felt a responsibility to keep that memorial candle burning, I was hesitant to break this last barrier of silence and question Survivors about the sexual abuse that they had experienced. They had undergone so many physical horrors that to add such an intrusion seemed like another assault. I wanted to respect the dignity of the Survivors who chose not to bring out this aspect of their nightmare for so long. I thought it would be humiliating to talk about their sexual abuse, in particular because it was more of an unspeakable, secretive part of their lives, in comparison with other forms of horrors endured that had been talked about more openly.

Susan: Some instances of sexual abuse were widely known, such as the public shaving of the body hair of concentration camp inmates and the exclusion of privacy. But such abuses were not specifically regarded as sexual abuse, but rather as part of the unrelenting terror and depersonalization of the Holocaust. Their immeasurable suffering made it easy to overlook the sexual abuse imbedded in so many of the Survivors' experiences. This aspect of their colossal torment needs to be told.

When we began work on this book, I was concerned that by focusing on sexual abuse we would be minimizing the horror of the Holocaust. Even the subtitle "Hell within Hell" connotes a type of equality between sexual abuse on the one hand and the boundless torture of the Holocaust on the other. I also didn't want to minimize the nightmare of sexual abuse. For me, one of the legacies of the Holocaust is the abhorrence of violence and intentional affliction of psychological pain. Nevertheless, the sexual abuse that the Survivors had experienced was within the context of the inexorable, dehumanizing terrors of the Holocaust itself, and in that sense it is incomparable and inseparable.

Rachel: You relate to the terror of the Holocaust as an entire entity; hence you consider the sexual abuse Jews suffered as inextricable from their total humiliation and torture. Many others view it that way too, and that's partly the reason why the sexual abuse of Survivors of the Holocaust has not been adequately recognized as an additional violent aspect of what they endured. Because I lived under the shadow of the Holocaust, it is easier for me to extract each separate type of abuse while regarding the full spectrum of what survivors suffered as a whole.

Holocaust Survivors who were sexually abused were dislocated from their country, family, friends, culture, humanity, and their own bodies. They were not connected to any place, anyone, or even to themselves; they were left with nothing and became the ultimate refugees, with no home or body to return to.

Susan: It does seem though that whether Survivors were sexually abused or not, the immense barbaric cruelty of the Holocaust belies those who casually say that some survived because of alleged individual attributes such as body strength, strong immune systems, the nature of their character, or creative thinking. Such claims minimize the truth: The Survivors were helpless in face of the atrocities of the Holocaust. Who lived and who didn't was overwhelmingly a matter of luck or coincidence.

Rachel: Your comments touch on something else. I hesitated to interview Survivors about their experiences of sexual abuse I did not want to secondarily go through the horrors and feel so helpless myself. My way of coping has been to move away from my feelings of helplessness and take action to help people overcome such feelings within themselves. Instead of feeling helpless myself, I help others. I developed this coping strategy early in life by my attempts to save my parents

Susan: You had to move away from these horrifying images and emotions because you have absorbed your parents' pain so intimately. I actually see this as giving you an advantage; you are closer to touching and understanding the unknowable. There is a chasm between me and the Survivors, because I can't grasp the massive dread and pain of the Holocaust. I feel cut off, disconnected from the Holocaust. This leaves me almost involuntarily in a position which allows me to minimize its horror because it is too extraordinarily excruciating to get my mind and heart around. I am always trying to get close enough to it to understand and feel more, so that it does not remain a virtual reality but it becomes real to me in the same way I believe it does for you.

Rachel: And my quest is to get away from it. A part of me is always in the grips of the Holocaust; so I work to keep away from being consumed by it. I don't look downward into the pit that is the Holocaust. I look up all the time and straight ahead, not to the sides and not to the back, in order not to get lost.

Susan: You look away, move away, and stay focused because you have a sense of that bottomless pit. And my feelings are available, ironically, because I don't have access to the full depths of what was felt and experienced. I've cried during the writing and research of this book project, touched by the terror, suffering, humanity, humiliation, courage, loss, and deprivation experienced and expressed by the Survivors. I have had traumatic reactions, too. For example, after working all day on a vignette, I took my usual evening walk down the streets of Haifa, but this time I felt fearful and reacted by being easily startled by sounds and passersby. During our work together, sometimes you would exclaim that I was tearful and that it was too sad for tears. Perhaps in our different ways we were both out of touch with the Holocaust. Because you had encountered it far more closely, you needed to look up and away and stay disconnected. I could look down into the pit, but the darkness prevented me from seeing its depths. Otherwise, I would have cried until I had no more tears.

Rachel: The Survivors' stories often go to the bottom of the pit, to a dead end without the possibility of major healing. You, who studied the Holocaust and are interested in how Survivors cope, can identify and empathize with them and react as a human being to their suffering. I, who had no choice but to live in the shadow of the Holocaust all my life, had to daily shield myself against my parents' pain and at the same time take on the role of the parent towards them and try to protect them and help them feel good about themselves as parents. I couldn't afford to empathize with the total helplessness Survivors experienced during the Holocaust. I needed to defend myself by dissociating, not from the information and knowledge in my possession, but from the emotions that I felt. But, emotions relating to the Holocaust still seeped in to the core of me. I studied child sexual abuse and made it one of my research agendas, probably because incidents of sexual abuse render children helpless. I sought to escape the helplessness of Survivors only to be drawn into the helplessness of victims of sexual abuse.

Susan: In order to emotionally survive you have dissociated yourself from the helpless feelings of Survivors. Similarly, victims of sexual abuse often dissociate to cope with the danger and trauma they experience. Dissociation has direct application to Jews during this post Holocaust period, or at the very least, it is an accurate metaphor for the splits this catastrophe has caused our people. The Holocaust separates living Jews from each other. Anti-Semitism may have been internalized, with some Jews converting and others rushing toward assimilation. Some Jews, such as many of those who lived in the Americas, didn't experience the Holocaust directly. Even the ripple effects extending to succeeding generations varied widely. We cannot all experience, comprehend, and react identically to such a monstrous, explosive, dislocating, wounding calamity. So it hinders our ability to share history, to communicate, and to support and validate each other. It makes community cohesion and understanding more difficult.

Rachel: Perhaps it has disconnected our people, but it also disconnected Survivors from their present lives.

Susan: The seven Survivors interviewed here were effective in their lives, often creating their own families, contributing to their communities, succeeding at their work, and adapting to new surroundings and even to different cultures and languages. It amazes me that they were able to come out of the inferno and often function at high levels, achieve so much, and give so much to others. In spite of all this, some didn't know if being alive was better than being dead. The deliberate, abundant, and sadistic cruelty broke lives; there is a limit, after all, to how much people can take. Some Survivors of other forms of traumas have revealed that after many years, they did succeed in integrating their experiences into their lives, gained personal power, and consequently felt that they could survive anything. Holocaust survivors have survived everything already, so it is different for them.

Rachel: They sometimes come to the realization that they lived but would have rather died. This leaves their children, the children of Holocaust Survivors, with a heavy burden, too. Their very birth and existence means that life won: Their parents won out over the Nazis. Yet their parents continually mourned the loss of their murdered family members and longed for them. They held deep unresolved yearnings to reunite with those they loved and lost. Sometimes, this left the second generation with feelings of helplessness and failure because they could not fulfill their ultimate role. They couldn't save their parents by filling the void left by the perished ones in their parents' hearts.

Survivors had encountered so much death during the Holocaust that many of their children sensed death as palpable. Some second-generation children could sense it secondhand and feel searing pain from the death of persons they had never known. These children could not touch their parents' deeply longing inner souls or comfort them. Consequently, they absorbed these "voids", and parts of their own souls died too. This partial deadening is manifested by their inability to feel joy, by controlling feelings, and by being ready to escape any intimacy before getting hurt. It is as if part of us will always virtually remain in the Holocaust.

REFERENCES

American Psychiatric Association. *Diagnostic and Statistical Manual of Mental Disorders* (1994) (4th edition). Washington, DC: Author.

Amir, M. & Lev-Wiesel, R. Time does not heal all wounds: Quality of life and psychological distress of people who survived the Holocaust as children 55 years later. (2003). *Journal of Traumatic Stress*, 16(3), 295—300.

Amnesty International. Updates. (2004). London: AI.

Amone-P'Olak, K. Psychological impact of war and sexual abuse on adolescent girls. (2005). *Northern Uganda Intervention*, 3(1), 33—45.

Amone-P'Olak, K. The impact of civil strife. (2003). *Assessment Report* (NUPSA). Marianum Press.

Bar-Tur, L. & Levy-Shiff, R. Holocaust review and bearing witness as a coping mechanism of an elderly Holocaust survivor. (1994). *Clinical Gerontologist: The Journal of Aging and Mental Health*, 14(3), 5—16.

Bass, E. & Davis, L. *The courage to heal*. (1988). New York: Row.

Bitton, L. E. & Jackson, E. *Coming of age in the Holocaust*. (1980). New York: Times Books.

Briere, J. *Therapy for adults molested as children: Beyond survival.* (1989). New York: Springer.

Briere, J. *Child Abuse Trauma: Theory and Treatment of the Lasting Effects.* (1992). London: Sage Publications.

Browne, A., & Finkelhor, D. Impact of child sexual abuse: A review of the literature. (1986). *Psychological Bulletin*, 99, 66—77.

Bruckner, D.F. & Johnson, P.E. Treatment for survivors of childhood sexual abuse. (1987). *Social Casework*, 87, 81—87.

Chodoff, P. Late effects of the concentration camp syndrome. (1963). *Archives of General Psychiatry*, 8, 323—333.

Chu, J. R. Rebuilding shuttered lives: The responsible treatment of complex posttraumatic and dissociative disorders. (1998). New York: John Wiley & Sons.

Courtois, C. A.. Recollections of sexual abuse: Treatment principles and guidelines. (1999). New York: W. W. Norton & Co.

Danieli, Y. The treatment and prevention of long-term effects and intergenerational transmission of victimization: A lesson from Holocaust survivors and their children. (1985). In C.F. Figley (Ed.), Trauma and its wake: The study and treatment of post-traumatic stress disorder (pp. 295-313). New York: Brunner/ Mazel.

REFERENCES

Dasberg, H. *Needs of Holocaust Survivors in Israel.* AMCHA, Jerusalem.

Davidson, S. (1972). The treatment of Holocaust survivors. (1990). In S. Davidson (Ed.), *Spheres of psychotherapeutic activity.* Jerusalem.

Derek, J. Mood disturbances among women clients sexually abused during childhood. (1989). *Journal of Interpersonal Violence,* 4(2), 122—133.

DiLillo et al. Retrospective assessment of childhood sexual and physical abuse. (2006). *Assessment,* 13, 297—312.

Draijer, N. & Langeland, W. Childhood trauma and perceived parental dysfunction in the etiology of dissociative symptoms in psychiatric inpatients. (1999). *The American Journal of Psychiatry,* 156(3), 379—385.

Farley, M. & Patsalides, B.M. Physical symptoms, posttraumatic stress disorder, and healthcare utilization of women with and without childhood physical and sexual abuse. (2001). *Psychological Reports,* 89(3), 595—606.

Finkelhor, D. Early and long term effects of child sexual abuse: An update. (1990). *Professional Psychology: Research and Practice,* 21, 325—330.

Fleming, J., Mullen, P.E., Sibthorpe, B., & Bammer, G. The long-term impact of childhood sexual abuse in Australian women. (1999). *Child Abuse & Neglect,* 23(2), 145—159

Foa, E.B. & Kozak, M.J. Emotional processing of fear: Exposure to corrective information. (1986). *Psychological Bulletin,* 99(1), 20—35.

Fraizier, P., Byrne, C., Glaser, T., Hurliman, E., Iwan, A., & Searles, L. Multiple traumas and PTSD among sexual assault survivors. (1997, August). Paper presented at the annual meeting of the American Psychological Association, Chicago, IL.

Gampel, Y. I was a Shoah child. (1992). *British Journal of Psychotherapy,* 8(4), 390—400.

Gold, S. N. Relationship between Childhood Sexual Abuse Characteristics and Dissociation among Women in Therapy. (1999). *Journal of Family Violence* 14(2), 157—171.

Herman, J. Trauma and recovery. (1992). New York: Basic Books.

Hoyt, S. L. The perception of danger cues in traumatized and nontraumatized populations. (2002). *Dissertation Abstracts International: Section B: The Sciences and Engineering,* 62(12—B), 5965.

Human Rights Watch, The Scars of Death: Children abducted by the Lord's Resistance Army in Uganda. (1997). Abducted and Abused: Human Rights Watch, New York.

Human Rights Watch, Abducted and Abused: Renewed Conflict in Northern Uganda. (July 2003).

Kendall-Tackett, K. A., Williams, L. M., & Finkelhor, D. Impact of sexual abuse on children: A review and synthesis of recent empirical studies. (1993). Psychological Bulletin, 113, 164—180.

Kendall-Tackett, K.A. & Marshall, R. Victimization and diabetes: An exploratory study. (1999). *Child Abuse & Neglect,* 23(6), 593—596.

Kendall-Tackett, K.A. How child sexual abuse harms relationships. (2002). *PsycCRITIQUES,* 47(2), 207—209.

Kestenberg, J., & Brenner, I. Children who survived the Holocaust: The role of rules and routines in the development of the superego. (1986). *International Journal of Psychoanalysis*, 67, 309—316.

Kestenberg, M., & Kestenberg, J.S. The sense of belonging and altruism in children who survived the Holocaust. (1988). *Psychoanalytic Review*, 75(4), 533—560.

Kilpartrick, D. G., Saunders, B. E., Amick-McMullen, A., & Best, C. L. Victim and crime factors associated with the development of crime-related posttraumatic stress disorder. (1989). *Behavior Therapy*, 20, 199—214.

Klein, H. Child victims of the Holocaust. (1974). *Journal of Clinical Child Psychology*, 2, 44—47.

Krell, R. Therapeutic value of documenting child survivors. (1986). *Annual Progress in Child Psychiatry and Child Development*, 281—288.

Krell, R. Child survivors of the Holocaust: strategies of adaptation. (1993). *Canadian Journal of Psychiatry*, 38, 384—389.

Krug, E.G., Mercy, J.A., Dahlberg, L.L., Zwi, A.B. The world report on violence and health. (2002). *The Lancet,* 360(9339), 1083—1088.

Krystal, J., Bremner, J. D., D'Souza, D. C., Anand, A., Southwick, S. M. and Charney, D. The Emerging Neurobiology of Dissociative States: Relevance to PTSD. (2000). in: Shalev, A., Yehuda, R. and McFarlane, A. C. (eds.) *International Handbook of Human Response to Trauma* (pp. 307—320). New York: Kluwer Academic/Plenum Publishers.

Landau, R. & Litwin ,H. The effects of extreme early stress in the very old age. (2000). *Journal of Traumatic Stress*, 13, 487—473 .

Lee, B. S. Holocaust survivors and internal strengths. (1988). *Journal of Humanistic psychology*, 28(1), 67—96.

Lederer, W. Persecution and compensation. (1965). *Archive Gen Psychiatry*, 8, 334.

Leserman, J. Sexual abuse history: Prevalence, health effects, mediators, and psychological treatment. (2005). *Psychosomatic Medicine*, 67(6), 906—915.

Lev-Wiesel, R. & Amir, M. Posttraumatic stress disorder symptoms, psychological distress, personal resources and quality of life in four groups of Holocaust child survivors. (2000). *Family Process*, 39(4), 445—460.

Lev-Wiesel, R., & Amir, M. Holocaust child survivors and child sexual abuse. (2005). *Journal of Child Sexual Abuse*, 14(2), 69—83.

Lev-Wiesel, R. Intergenerational transmission of trauma across three generations: A preliminary study. (2007). *Qualitative Social Work: Research and Practice*, 6(1), 75—94

Lorenzer, A. Some observations on the latency symptoms in patients suffering from persecution sequelae. (1968). *International Journal of Psychoanalysis*, 49, 316.

Lynton, S. M. The effects of multiple trauma: An explanatory study of daughters of Jewish Holocaust survivors who themselves experienced childhood physical and/or sexual abuse. (1998). *Dissertation Abstracts International: The sciences and Engineering*, 59(6—B), 3065.

REFERENCES

Midgley, N. Child Dissociation and its Roots in Adulthood. (2002). in: V. Sinason, (Ed.), *Attachment, Trauma and Multiplicity* (pp. 37—51). New York: Brunner-Routeledge.

Moeller, T. P., Bachmann, G. A., & Moeller, J. R. The combined effects of physical, sexual and emotional abuse during childhood: Long-term health consequences for women. (1993). *Child Abuse and Neglect*, 17, 623—640.

Moskovitz, S., & Krell, R. Child survivors of the Holocaust: Psychological adaptations to survival. (1990). *Israel Journal of Psychiatry and Related sciences*, 27(2), 81—91.

Nathan, T.S., Ettinger, L., & Winnik, H. Z. A psychiatrist study of survivors of the Nazi Holocaust. (1964). *Israel Annals of Psychiatry*, 2, 47.

Neumann, D. A., Houskamp, B. M., Pollock, V. E., & Briere, J. The long-term sequelae of childhood sexual abuse in women: A meta-analytic review. (1996). *Child Maltreatment*, 1, 6—16.

Niederland, W. Psychiatric disorders among persecution victims. (1964). *Journal of Nervous Disorders*, 52, 139—458.

Nijenhuis, E.R.S, Van Dyck, R., Ter Kuile, M.M, Mourits, M.J.E., Spinhoven, P., Van der Hart, O. Evidence for associations among somatoform dissociation, psychological dissociation and reported trauma in patients with chronic pelvic pain. (2003). *Journal of Pyschosomatic Obstetrics & Gynecology*, 24(2), 87 - 98.

Peleikis, D. E., Mykletum, A., & Dahl, A. A. The relative influence of childhood sexual abuse and other family background risk factors on adults adversities in female outpatients treated for anxiety disorders and depression. (2003). *Child Abuse &Neglect,* 28, 61—76.

Pennebaker, J.W. Confession, inhibition and disease. (1989). in: L. Berkowitz, (Ed.) *Advances in Experimental Social Psychology* (pp. 211–244). New York: Academic Press.

Pennebaker, J.W. & Chung, C.K. Expressive writing, emotional upheavals and health. (2007). in: Friedman, H.S. & Cohen-Silver, R. (eds.) *Foundations of Health Pyscology* (pp 263 - 284). New York: Oxford University Press.

Pikarinen, U., Saisto, T., Schei, B., Swahnberg, K., Halmesmäki, E. Experiences of Physical and Sexual Abuse and their Implications for Current Health. (2007). *Obstetrics & Gynecology* 109 (5), 1116—1122

Putnam, F.W. Dissociative phenomena. Dissociative disorders: A clinical review. (1993). Spiegel, D. (Ed.) *Dissociative disorders: A clinical review* (pp. 1—16). Baltimore, MD, US: The Sidran Press.

Randolph M.E. & Reddy, D.M. Sexual functioning in women with chronic pelvic pain: The impact of depression, support, and abuse. (2006). *Journal of Sex Research*, 43(1), 38—45.

Reissing, E.D., Binik, Y.M., Khalifé, S., Cohen, D. & Amsel, R. Etiological correlates of vaginismus: Sexual and physical abuse, Sexual knowledge sexual self-schema and relationship adjustment. (2003). *Journal of Sex & Marital Therapy*, 29(1), 47—59.

Resnick, H. S., Kilpatrick, D. G., Dansky, B. S., Saunders, B. E., & Best, C. L. Prevalence of civilian trauma and PTSD in a representative national sample of women. (1993). *Journal of Consulting and Clinical Psychology*, 16, 984—991.

Rind, B., Tromovitch, P., & Bauserman, R. A meta-analytic examination of assumed properties of child sexual abuse using college samples. (1998). *Psychological Bulletin*, 124, 22—53.

Ringelheim, J. The split between gender and the Holocaust. (1998). in D. Ofer, & L.J. Weitzman (Eds.), *Women in the Holocaust*, (pp. 340—350). New Haven: Yale University Press.

Robinson, S., Rapaport Bar Sever, M., & Rapaport, J. The present state of people who survived the Holocaust as children. (1994). *Acta Psychiatrica Scandinavica*, 89, 242—245.

Rodrigues-Srednicki, O. Childhood sexual abuse, dissociation and adult self-destructive behavior. (2001). *Journal of Child Sexual Abuse*, 10(3), 75—90.

Royse, D., Rompf, E.L., & Dohooper, S.S. Childhood trauma and adult life satisfaction in a random sample. (1991). *Psychological Reports*, 69(3), 1227—1231.

Russel, D. E. H. *The secret trauma: Incest in the women.* (1986). New York: Basic Books.

Shalev, A.Y. Post-traumatic stress disorder: A biopsychological perspective. (1993). *Israel Journal of Psychiatry and Related Sciences*, 30(2), 102—109

Shalev, A.Y. Acute to chronic: Etiology and pathophysiology of PTSD—A biopsychosocial approach. (1997). Fullerton, C.S., Ursano, R.J. (Eds.) *Post-traumatic stress disorder: Acute and long-term responses to trauma and disaster, Progress in psychiatry series*, No. 51 (pp. 209—240). Washington, DC, US: American Psychiatric Association.

Shengold, L. Soul murder: The effects of childhood abuse and deprivation. (1989). New Haven, CT, US: Yale University Press.

Silberg, J. L. Dissociative Symptomatology in Children and Adolescents as Displayed on Psychological Testing. (1998). *Journal of Personality Assessment*, 71(3), 421—439.

Simpson T.L. & Miller, W.R. Concomitance between childhood sexual and physical abuse and substance use problems: A review. (2002). *Clinical Psychology Review*, 22(1), 27—77.

Somer, L. & Somer, E. Psychodynamic perspectives on art-work in dissociative identity disorder. (1997). *Sihot/Dialogue: Israel Journal of Psychotherapy*, 11(3), 183—194.

Swartz, T.S. An investigation of the impact of childhood sexual abuse on developing object relations as a function of age at onset of abuse. (2002). *Dissertation Abstracts International: Section B: The Sciences and Engineering*, 63(6—B), 3027.

Tec, N. A historical perspective tracing the history of the hidden child experience. (1993). in: J. Marks (Ed.), *The hidden children: The secret survivors of the Holocaust* (pp. 273—291). New York: Fawcett Columbia.

Ullman, S. E. & Filipas, H. H. Predictors of PTSD symptoms severity and social reactions in sexual assault victims. (2001). *Journal of Traumatic Stress*,

14(2), 369—389.
UNICEF. *Northern Uganda Psychosocial Needs Assessment Report.* (1998). (NUPSA). Marianum Press: Kisubi, Uganda.
Valent, P. Documented childhood trauma (Holocaust): Its sequel and applications to other traumas. (1995). *Psychiatry, Psychology and Law*, 2, 81—89.
Van Den Bosch, L. M. C., Verheul, R., Langwland, W., & Van Den Brink, W. Trauma, dissociation, and posttraumatic stress disorder in female borderline patients with and without substance abuse problems. (2003). *Australian and New Zealand Journal of Psychiatry*, 37(5), 549—555.
Vardi, D. *Memorial candles.* (1991). Jerusalem: Keter (Hebrew).
Williams, L.M., Finkelhor, D., Kendall-Tackett, K.A. Impact of sexual abuse on children: A review and synthesis of recent empirical studies. (1993). *Psychological Bulletin*, 113(1), 164—180
Winnicot, D. W. *Maturational processes and facilitating environment.* (1965). New York: International Universities Press.
Yehuda, R., Kahana, B., Binder-Brynes, K., Southwick, S., Mason, J. W., & Giller, E. Low urinary cortisol excretion in Holocaust survivors with posttraumatic stress disorder. (1995). *American Journal of Psychiatry*, 152, 982—986.
Yehuda, R., Schmeidler, J., Siever, L. J., Binder-Brynes, K., & Elkin A. Individual differences in posttraumatic stress symptom profiles in Holocaust survivors in concentration camps or in hiding. (1997). *Journal of Traumatic Stress*, 10(3), 453—463.
Zelikovsky, N. & Lynn, S.J. Childhood psychological and physical abuse: Psychopathology, dissociation, and Axis I diagnosis. (2002). *Journal of Trauma & Dissociation*, 3(3), 27—58.
Zurbriggen, E.L. & Freyd, J.J. The link between child sexual abuse and risky sexual behavior: The role of dissociative tendencies, information-processing effects, and consensual sex decision mechanisms. From child sexual abuse to adult sexual risk: Trauma, revictimization, and intervention. (2004). in Koenig, L.J., Doll, L.S., O'Leary, A., Pequegnat, W. (Eds.) *From child sexual abuse to adult sexual risk: Trauma, revictimization, and intervention*, (pp. 135—157). Washington, DC, US: American Psychological Association, xv, 346 pp

ABOUT THE AUTHORS

Rachel Lev-Wiesel, Ph.D., a Professor and Chair of the Graduate School of Creative Art Therapies, University of Haifa, in Israel, has published more than one hundred scientific papers and chapters, and five books on issues such as the long term effects of the Holocaust, intergenerational transmission of trauma, and child sexual abuse. She belongs to the second generation of descendants of Holocaust survivors.

Susan Weinger, Ph.D., Professor of Social Work at Western Michigan University, Kalamazoo, Michigan, in the United States, focuses on gender issues, poverty and multicultural sensitivity in her teaching, research and service activities.

www.ingramcontent.com/pod-product-compliance
Lightning Source LLC
Chambersburg PA
CBHW052135300426
44116CB00010B/1908